EARLY YEARS INCLUSIVE PRACTICE FOR CHILDREN WITH SEND

Have you seen a rise in the number of children with SEND in your setting? Are you concerned about how to give them the best start alongside other children? Based on four decades of experience with a range of settings and children with SEND, this book takes you through the key practices that will enable you to be truly inclusive.

Drawing from work undertaken by Dingley's Promise, a national charity striving to provide every child with the best start, chapters explore how we can support the early identification of need and provide a tailored response for individual children. The book considers a range of issues that have been raised by settings as barriers to inclusion, as well as crucial aspects such as discussions with parents, home learning and well-being. With real-life case studies from the playroom to bring theory to life, questions to encourage reflection and a wealth of practical strategies, this book ensures that every setting has the knowledge, confidence and support they need to drive meaningful early years inclusion for young children with SEND.

Early Years Inclusive Practice for Children with SEND offers a wider understanding of what good inclusive practice is, ensuring that children with SEND have the best early experience they can. It is a must-have resource for all early years practitioners and managers to keep in their setting, and refer back to as they work inclusively and to help them with inductions of new staff to their setting.

Catherine Mole, MBE, is CEO of Dingley's Promise, UK. Catherine is passionate about equity and inclusion for all children and young people with disabilities and was awarded an MBE in 2011 for her work with disadvantaged children.

EARLY YEARS INCLUSIVE PRACTICE FOR CHILDREN WITH SEND

Giving Every Child the Best Start

Edited by Catherine Mole MBE

Routledge
Taylor & Francis Group

LONDON AND NEW YORK

Designed cover image: Peter McClintock

First published 2026
by Routledge
4 Park Square, Milton Park, Abingdon, Oxon OX14 4RN

and by Routledge
605 Third Avenue, New York, NY 10158

Routledge is an imprint of the Taylor & Francis Group, an informa business

© 2026 selection and editorial matter, Catherine Mole MBE; individual chapters, the contributors

The right of Catherine Mole MBE to be identified as the author of the editorial material, and of the authors for their individual chapters, has been asserted in accordance with sections 77 and 78 of the Copyright, Designs and Patents Act 1988.

All rights reserved. No part of this book may be reprinted or reproduced or utilised in any form or by any electronic, mechanical, or other means, now known or hereafter invented, including photocopying and recording, or in any information storage or retrieval system, without permission in writing from the publishers.

For Product Safety Concerns and Information please contact our EU representative GPSR@taylorandfrancis.com. Taylor & Francis Verlag GmbH, Kaufingerstraße 24, 80331 München, Germany.

Trademark notice: Product or corporate names may be trademarks or registered trademarks, and are used only for identification and explanation without intent to infringe.

British Library Cataloguing-in-Publication Data
A catalogue record for this book is available from the British Library

ISBN: 9781032899183 (hbk)
ISBN: 9781032899138 (pbk)
ISBN: 9781003545309 (ebk)

DOI: 10.4324/9781003545309

Typeset in Interstate
by Deanta Global Publishing Services, Chennai, India

Access the support materials: www.routledge.com/9781032899138

CONTENTS

	Editor and contributing authors	vii
	Foreword	ix
1	Introduction to inclusive practice *Meggie Fisher*	1
2	Leadership and management of inclusion *Meggie Fisher and Lee Friend*	14
3	Early identification *Louise White*	24
4	Monitoring and assessment *Meggie Fisher*	37
5	Voice of the child *Abi Preston-Rees*	54
6	The inclusive team *Lee Friend*	68
7	Family partnerships *Megan Harper*	81
8	Intersections of inclusion *Meggie Fisher*	96
9	Enabling environments *Megan Harper*	104
10	Behaviours that challenge *Abi Preston-Rees*	115

11	Transitions for children with SEND	136
	Abi Preston-Rees	
12	Well-being in early years	147
	Louise White	

In conclusion — *159*
Index — *161*

EDITOR AND CONTRIBUTING AUTHORS

Editor

Catherine Mole, MBE, has been a charity leader for over 25 years and is passionate about equity and inclusion for children and young people with disabilities. She became the Chief Executive of Dingley's Promise in 2015 and has grown the organisation from a small local charity to a national one that delivers training and influences policy alongside its core local support services. She was awarded an MBE in 2011 for her work with disadvantaged children, and today is a mentor for ACEVO, a national speaker, and an advisor to a range of governmental and non-governmental bodies around early years SEND inclusion. In 2025 she received the Third Sector Charity CEO Award recognising her contribution to the sector and drive towards inclusion in early years.

Contributing authors

Meggie Fisher has a BA(Hons) in Early Childhood and has worked in early years for over a decade championing support for children with SEND and developing inclusive practice. Having worked for many mainstream early years providers, she is now the Head of Quality for Dingley's Promise, working closely with the specialist centres to ensure they are delivering high-quality teaching and excellent inclusive practice and support for children. She is passionate about creating the best start for every child, recognising the unique opportunity we have to build strong foundations for lifelong learning and celebrating each child as an individual.

Lee Friend is a highly experienced and passionate early years professional who has worked in early years and education for nearly two decades. He is currently the Chief Operating Officer at Dingley's Promise. He is dedicated to creating inclusive environments, removing barriers for children and their families, and working together to give every child the very best start in life. Lee believes that there is a one-size-fits-one approach to supporting children with SEND and is passionate about supporting best practice to enable children to reach their full potential with the support and confidence they need.

Megan Harper is a qualified early years teacher with an MA in education who has worked in early years for 18 years. She is currently a Regional Operations and Quality Manager at Dingely's Promise. She is passionate about creating inclusive environments, taking inspiration from hygge, Scandinavian and nature-based practices. She is dedicated to breaking down barriers for children and their families. Meg believes that a holistic approach to supporting families is key and that all children deserve to feel safe and loved in their settings, to enable them to thrive.

Abi Preston-Rees has been supporting children and young people with special educational needs and disabilities for 22 years. She has worked as a Centre Manager and Training Lead at Dingley's Promise. She has gained knowledge and experience through working alongside families and professionals in specialist school and nursery settings, as well as providing respite care within her own home for children with SEND since 2010. She is the SEND Governor for a local primary school and an independent Foster Panel member. She has a level 5 in Early Years Management, specialising in specialist settings.

Louise White is a qualified early years practitioner and has contributed to some chapters of this book by drawing on her experience from 17 years of working for Dingley's Promise to help shape its message. Louise has worked as an apprentice, practitioner, Centre Manager and now as a Regional Operations and Quality Manager at Dingley's Promise. Being part of this project has been a meaningful and rewarding journey. Louise believes in Dingley's Promise mission of giving children the best start and the beginning of this journey is to connect with the families and children, building that trust and care for the learning to follow naturally

FOREWORD

This book is the culmination of 42 years of work supporting children with SEND in the early years to thrive at Dingley's Promise specialist early years SEND Centres. Our Centres work with groups of children who have a wide range of needs, meaning that strategies for including children are critical to our success. In 2015, approximately 35% of the children we supported transitioned to the mainstream, but ten years later around 70% of our children were transitioning to the mainstream. This was not an accidental change, but the result of carefully planned changes in the way we worked. It began by sharing provision with mainstream settings, followed by the introduction of our Entry Exit pathway (EEP). The EEP aligned the child's development, the feelings and confidence of the family, and the skills and confidence of the child's next educational setting. It was not only important in helping our Centres plan the movement of children to the mainstream, but also served to increase the confidence of families in the process and empower them to see a positive future for their child. We are now in a situation where children transition to the mainstream when they and their families are ready, and when we have worked with the receiving setting to give them the appropriate strategies to successfully support the individual child to thrive.

What underpins this huge change is an inclusive mindset that is embedded at Dingley's Promise and is critical for any setting that wants to have meaningful inclusion for children with SEND. This mindset includes the following aspects.

- Parents are experts in their children – but want honesty.

Dingley's Promise research (2025) showed that early years educators are the professionals that families of children with SEND in the early years trust the most. We are in a trusted position, and so we have to work in partnership with families. We have to ensure that we inform them of every part of the process, that we share documents with them so that they understand what their rights and entitlements are, and we have to be brave and have difficult conversations with them. Parents tell us that while conversations can be challenging, and it may take them time to adjust to information they were not expecting, they want us to have those conversations with them. We absolutely must recognise that they are the experts on their child, and believe what they say, but we must also give them our professional opinions, so that they are fully informed and can make the decisions that are right for them and their family.

- One-to-one support often does not lead to the best outcomes for the child.

A common belief is that the more support a child has, the better it is for them – especially if they have additional needs. However, the use of a one-to-one adult support can also be seen to have a negative impact on child outcomes. In general, adult support should be used to enhance ratios and to help with short, specific activities. A very small number of children may need one-to-one adult support if there is a significant risk of harm to themselves or to other children, but otherwise we should be relying on strong inclusive practice with children supported to play and learn alongside their peers.

- Behaviour is communication.

A child in distress or trying to make you aware of how they are feeling may display behaviours that in the past would have been labelled as "bad". Truly inclusive practitioners understand that all behaviour is communication, and that rather than try to force this behaviour to stop, we need to look at what the child is trying to communicate. The only way to reduce behaviours that educators may find 'difficult' is to have a deep understanding of the child and a curiosity about how they are feeling and what they are trying to tell you.

- Some inclusion is better than none.

Some educators feel that if a child is going to end up in special education in the future, it is better for them to go there sooner rather than have to have another transition later on. We believe that we have to be positive about the future and not jump to conclusions about children's life outcomes before we are sure. In our experience, there are many children whose families were told they would never succeed in the mainstream, but with the right support and strategies in place, they have thrived alongside their peers. We also know there is evidence that some experience of inclusion is better than none when it comes to life outcomes, and so even a short time in the mainstream where a child is thriving alongside their peers, is better for their development than going straight to special education.

- Good inclusive practice helps every child.

It is important to understand that good inclusive practice benefits every child in a setting – not just the children with SEND. Strong inclusive practice is high-quality teaching, and what is good for children with SEND enables every child to learn effectively. Some settings worry that parents will complain if they need to spend time meeting the needs of specific children, but with strong inclusive strategies, there is less reliance on one-to-one adult working and all children benefit from clear strategies which enhance learning.

- Inclusion is everyone's responsibility.

The role of SENCO can be lonely and can also become dominated by paperwork and meetings rather than delivering support directly to children. It is critical that inclusion is not just the job of the SENCO. The whole team, including the leadership, should be knowledgeable and confident in delivering inclusion to all children. Not only does this take the pressure off the SENCO and support the well-being of the team, but it means that families are reassured that even when the SENCO is not there, they know their child will be supported effectively.

- Every child is an individual.

While this may seem like an obvious statement in line with the EYFS notion of the unique child, it is important to note a specific angle on this. Some educators, once they have supported a child with a particular diagnosis, seem to think that they then know how to support the next child who attends their setting with the same diagnosis. It is critical to always remember that regardless of diagnosis, every child is an individual, and it is our job as educators to understand that child deeply and tailor our strategies to their needs.

- Celebratory approach.

Finally, the importance of the celebratory approach cannot be underestimated. We must celebrate every achievement of our children – no matter how big or small. For children with SEND and their families, we must focus on what they are able to do and what their strengths are rather than stating what they can't do. We must also be very careful that when we help children to progress, we are honouring the way they are and the way they want to do things. For example, forcing a neurodivergent child to make eye contact when it is uncomfortable for them is not helping their development, but rather seeking to make them conform to a neurotypical way of behaving. Truly inclusive educators never see a child as someone with 'delays' and 'deficits' that need to be "fixed". Rather, they are professionals who understand that every child will have a unique learning journey, with progress and styles of play that are celebrated.

Settings have told us that one of the key barriers to supporting more children with SEND is the lack of high-quality training for staff to access. Many early years educators worry that they cannot meet the needs of children and therefore wonder if they are the best place for children with SEND. This book is an important resource that you can keep in your setting and refer to regularly to support your practice. You should also check the Dingley's Promise website regularly (www.dingley.org.uk) where we post the most up-to-date information, formats, and resources that can be used to include children with SEND and further develop the quality of inclusive practice.

You may also want to look at the Dingley's Promise inclusion training programme, which offers short courses in key areas mentioned in this book. In many areas across England, you can access the courses for free through funded programmes. You can check your eligibility here: www.dingley.org.uk/training/

From a national perspective, Dingley's Promise will continue to gather the views of families, settings and local authorities, and use these to lobby government to improve support for inclusion in the early years. We recognise the challenges faced by providers related to funding, recruitment and retention, and want to offer inclusive solutions to these issues. If there is information or guidance that would help you, or if you would like Dingley's Promise to represent your views to decision makers, please do get in touch with us.

I hope that you can use this book to make sure as many children as possible can thrive in your setting.

Catherine Mole, MBE, Chief Executive

1
Introduction to inclusive practice

Meggie Fisher

> **KEY DEFINITIONS**
>
> Inclusion: A situation where everyone is actively included, supported and celebrated alongside their peers.
> Equality: Treating everybody the same, ensuring they have the same opportunities and support.
> Equity: Giving every person an equal chance to succeed by giving them the appropriate support, which is different according to individual needs.
> Reasonable Adjustments: A legal obligation to implement changes to ensure someone's disability does not put them at a disadvantage compared with others.
> Ordinarily Available Provision: As set out by your local authority, a range of practices and opportunities which should be available to support all children, especially those with SEND.

Introduction

Recognising, understanding and implementing effective inclusive practice is vital to ensuring all children are able to access and engage in play and learning. A passion to engage with all children is the best starting point to develop your practice and your setting to promote inclusion. This chapter will explore how to get started with your inclusive practice, guidance and regulations in place to promote inclusion, and how you can implement different strategies to engage and support children with a range of needs. It is important that through your journey into inclusive practice that you remember your children may need support across a variety of needs - some more prevalent than others. Some children you work with may have a formal diagnosis and others may be at the beginning of their diagnosis journey, or just need some additional support for a period of time. To deliver effective inclusion, you should recognise each child for who they are in that moment and provide support that meets their needs; each child will be different, and one child with sensory or physical needs may not benefit from the same strategies as another. Being confident to try, evaluate and change course through your graduated approach is vital to providing an approach that supports each individual child effectively (Figure 1.1).

Getting started

Inclusion is the practice of enabling everyone to feel welcome and valued within your provision and enabling them to all join and participate in any and all experiences on offer. Inclusive practice is fundamental to creating an environment in which all children are able to engage and thrive. A whole team approach and commitment to inclusion is key to ensuring that this happens, and you should consider the vision and leadership of a setting, the role of educators, the environment that you create, and the transitions children experience. It is important to recognise the need for consistency when promoting inclusion, especially when applying teaching practices and strategies. When everyone working in your provision is confident and secure in their understanding of why they are doing things, they are more able to commit to these practices and embed your ethos and vision. To support this commitment and develop an inclusive mindset, it is important to recognise and discuss why inclusion should be one of your leading values. All children deserve the opportunity to reach their full potential, and there are a variety of documents and legislation to help you understand your role and ways in which you can promote inclusion.

For children with SEND, their environment can have a long-lasting impact upon their feelings of belonging and aspiration; the influence of the provision's ethos and attitudes of their peers and educators is highly influential. Promoting and supporting inclusion alongside meeting a child's SEND needs, has a huge impact on the child's mental health and wellbeing. It recognises the child's needs and looks at how the environment can be adapted to better include them, rather than how the child should be changed to fit the current environment. This change in mindset opens a world of possibilities for the child as it promotes

Figure 1.1 Educator and child engaging through intensive interaction

their differences as something to be celebrated and accepted rather than a deficit that should be changed.

Inclusion supports and values the child alongside their peers, showing them that they are unique in their strengths and that they are as much a part of the group as everyone else. These messages are important for life-long learning and inclusion, for both the child with SEND and their peers. Teaching children self-worth allows them to hold onto this mindset as they grow older and interact with more of society, throughout their years of education as well as into the adult world. By teaching inclusively to all children from an early age, they are more likely to hold onto these values as they grow, bringing greater acceptance and support to the world around them and building a better future for all.

Where interactions, relationships and environments are positive and nurturing, children with SEND are more likely to feel they belong and can thrive in the provision. Therefore, the fundamentals of inclusion should be in place prior to individualised targeted provision.

The fundamentals of inclusion:

- Inclusive vision and values that are woven through policy and practice.
- High ambitions for all children.
- An understanding of "Ordinarily Available Provision" requirements within your local authority.
- An understanding and application of the duty to make "Reasonable Adjustments".
- Prioritising autonomy and ensuring children with SEND are represented throughout the provision.
- Positive relationships between educators and peers with inclusive teaching practices embedded.

Potential barriers to inclusion:

- Lack of understanding of what inclusion means.
- Not taking the time to establish the fundamentals of inclusion within your provision.
- Educators find change difficult or prefer "the way things have always been done".
- A lack of collaborative working across all educators.
- A lack of awareness of local authority support.
- Over-reliance on additional funding to "solve the problem".
- Poor induction for new team members to understand the inclusive vision and values.

The fundamentals of your inclusive practice should be established and promoted every day as part of your standard offer. In doing this, you set a foundation of consistent inclusion where all children, families and team members feel valued and recognised. You can find additional support when creating your provision by referring to your local authority's Ordinarily Available Provision (OAP) document, which will set out their expectations for what you should be providing to all children as high-quality teaching and how this should also support children with emerging and identified needs. In addition to this, you should also consider and plan for any Reasonable Adjustments you may make, should children need specialist support.

You may choose to think of this as your universal offer, targeted offer and specialist offer.

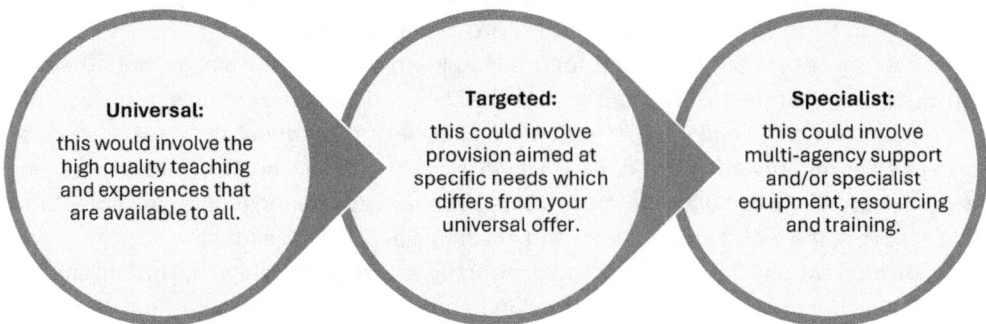

Universal: this would involve the high quality teaching and experiences that are available to all.

Targeted: this could involve provision aimed at specific needs which differs from your universal offer.

Specialist: this could involve multi-agency support and/or specialist equipment, resourcing and training.

Ordinarily Available Provision and Reasonable Adjustments

Ordinarily Available Provision sets out a universal set of expectations about the provision and practice that is expected in all early years settings for all children and young people with SEND. Ordinarily Available Provision is also in all educational settings. You should be aware of the OAP document in place within your local authority and familiarise yourself with the content relevant to your early years provision. This is what a parent or carer can expect to see or access as ordinarily available for their child without the need to have a referral submitted or seek further support externally. It is vital that families are made aware of OAP and what this means for their child as many parents and carers of children with SEND may not realise that their child has the same entitlement to early education as others. By making them aware that elements of support are not "extra" but are a part of a setting's standard offer, they become more confident in a setting's ability to support their child provide their child with the opportunity to access their early education.

A familiar element of a local authority's OAP is the high-quality teaching children receive. High-quality teaching considers the needs of all children within your setting, which then informs planning and delivery to make learning accessible for all. This should consist of a range of additional strategies or interventions which, when paired with high-quality teaching, will have a positive impact on the learning and development of all children, but particularly those with SEND. This may include teaching methods or actions of educators to promote engagement and interaction, considerations for the environment to reduce distraction, or being sensitive to sensory needs and making adjustments accordingly.

You may find that additional adjustments should be made to your provision or practice to enable children with SEND to participate in activities and to support their educational journey. The term "Reasonable Adjustments" applies specifically to changes made to support children with a disability, but it is often practically implemented to support all children with SEND. You have a duty to provide Reasonable Adjustments to meet the needs of children within your setting in accordance with the Equality Act 2010.

- First duty: altering or adjusting "provision, criteria, or practices" - which ecompassess mainly the way things are done in the setting.

- Second duty: to make reasonable adjustments to physical features of the building, such as: building or installing a ramp to improve accessibility.

- Third duty: is to provide "auxiliary aids and services" which includes the provision of equipment, advice and services.

The first requirement involves altering or adjusting "provisions, criteria or practices" – which encompasses mainly the way things are done within the setting, of which this is largely addressed through effective Ordinarily Available Provision. However, you may also need to consider if the needs of a child are being met within your standard practices with respect to ratios, rooms and staffing arrangements. Think about quiet spaces for children, Key Person allocation, visual aids and the training of you and your teams.

The second requirement is a duty to make Reasonable Adjustments to the physical features of the building. You may need to build or purchase a ramp to support accessibility, adjust lighting to enhance visibility or reduce flickering, or ensure the signage is clear. We need to consider more than just ensuring that there is an exit, think about the whole environment: is it accessible and accommodating to a range of needs.

The third requirement is to provide "auxiliary aids and services", which includes the provision of equipment, advice or support. You can gain further advice from the specialist health professionals working with a child about equipment that would be beneficial and where this can be sourced. This may sometimes include the provision of one-to-one support, but only if deemed the best option for the child. It can help to reach out to your local authority team, as they may be able to provide funding to support the purchase or hire of specialist equipment to support children's individual needs. Some families may also be entitled to financial aid to support the purchase of specialist equipment or make adjustments for their child. Knowing how to signpost to and support families with this information can make a huge impact on the child's quality of life and their family's confidence in supporting them.

Putting it into practice

Within your preschool room, you have three children with identified speech and language needs. One has the involvement of a speech and language therapist and the other two have been recently identified and are beginning to receive support within the setting. A new child is due to start in your preschool room who is partially deaf and wears hearing aids.

> When considering how inclusive your environment is for these children, you establish that 50% of the team working in this room are Makaton trained and confident in its use; the resources, all have clear photographic labels, all team members have participated in communication training within the last year, and there is a visual timetable on display. With this in mind, you are confident that the children will be able to access the resources and understand the routine and instructions given by the team. To further enhance your inclusive provision, you may wish to train or further expose the team who are not confident in using Makaton or other communication strategies. This could be achieved through the provision of lanyards with key visual symbols for ease and accessibility when showing and demonstrating instructions, or by reviewing what auditory stimulation is present, such as noise levels or background music, so that you can take steps to reduce these distractions for children learning to use spoken language.
>
> You may feel that some Reasonable Adjustments should be made to further support the child to access communication in the nursery environment. It is important to discuss with the family what works well for them at home and involve other professionals already working with this child. It may be ideal to utilise funds to purchase a microphone transmitter that is compatible with the child's hearing aids and teach the team how best to use this when the child is in the setting.

The graduated approach: a framework for support

When SEND or other needs are identified, it is crucial to follow a structured approach to intervention. The *graduated approach* is a framework designed to ensure support is planned, implemented, and reviewed effectively, in line with the expectations of the SEN Code of Practice. It follows the *Assess, Plan, Do, Review* cycle.

1. **Assess:** This involves gathering detailed information about the child through observations, specialist input, and family perspectives. Educators must assess the child's strengths, challenges, and the environmental factors that might influence their learning.
2. **Plan:** Based on the assessment, clear, specific targets are set for the child. These targets should be SMART (Specific, Measurable, Achievable, Relevant, Time-bound), and a plan is made to outline the interventions and strategies to be used.
3. **Do:** This phase involves implementing the planned interventions consistently and adapting them as necessary to meet the child's needs.
4. **Review:** Regular reviews are essential to assess whether the interventions are working and whether any changes are necessary. This should involve the educators, family, and specialists working together to monitor progress and adjust strategies.

To effectively support children's development, it is important to think reflectively about what opportunities we are providing them and how this is impacting their learning. Understanding and recognising which teaching strategies and resources children respond best to, is vital to developing ongoing, consistent support which meets their needs. The graduated approach is a simple reflective cycle that supports our thinking around the support we are implementing.

The power of the graduated approach lies in the ability to reflect and adapt to ensure you are making the environment and teaching practices accessible for the child's needs. It encourages you to think about the child's strengths and interests and utilise these when planning their access to your curriculum. Combining the graduated approach with strong Ordinarily Available Provision will create an environment in which children with SEND can be supported and included within a mainstream setting.

The graduated approach is a collaborative reflective model and works best when the team around the child works together to set out planned support and any specific resources or experience which will aid a child's development. Strong partnership working with the family and other external professionals enables you to consider the child's needs from a range of perspectives and build a picture of consistent support to enable the child to thrive in their environments.

Putting it into practice

Assess

Aaron is 2 years old. Through observing and interacting with Aaron, you know that he enjoys musical experiences, moving his head to the beat when music is played and watching closely when his key person sings and signs different nursery rhymes. He also smiles and laughs when he can crawl into the sandpit and often gestures for help to go on the slide. When completing a developmental assessment, you recognise his strengths in communication, using single words and gestures to communicate and his confidence when engaging with his peers and familiar adults. You also recognise the challenges he is experiencing with his gross motor skills, particularly limited mobility. You have a copy of Aaron's latest assessment with his physiotherapist, and you speak to his parents to ensure you have captured the skills and frustrations he demonstrates at home.

Plan

In collaboration with the setting SENCO and Aaron's parents, you discuss what support you are going to implement to help Aaron with his next stages of development. This conversation needs to consider recommendations from his physiotherapist, his interests and strengths, and how these can be used to promote further learning.

You determine that now that Aaron is confidently able to crawl/slide across a flat surface, you will implement new challenges to increase his core stability and work towards moving up and down steps. With Aaron's interest in music, you will use music and movement sessions to model to Aaron different ways to move his body, including waving arms, leaning from side to side, and lying flat and kicking his legs in the air, as these will increase his core stability. You also decide that his interest in the slide can be a strong motivator to support his exploration of steps. You can utilise a wide crate to make a more accessible step up to the slide, which Aaron should be able to crawl onto.

Do

You ensure that multiple times a week you engage Aaron and his peers in a music and movement session and begin to see his confidence increasing, particularly in leaning from side to side from a sitting position. He laughs during The Hokey-Pokey and has started to wiggle when you play The Flight of the Bumblebee.

You have tried to support him with the step up to the slide; however, you have realised that this is still quite a large step, and he needs to develop awareness of going up and over at a lower level before he can get to the slide. You immediately adjust this by starting with crawling up and over your legs as an initial challenge.

Review

After several weeks, you meet to discuss the progress you have seen with Aaron's development and can see his confidence in moving his body has grown. Whilst initially he could not engage in the step up to the slide, you were able to support him in lifting his arms and legs to crawl up and over your legs, and when his confidence grew, you moved back to the crate and, with support he was able to pull himself onto the crate, where he then gestured and said "up" to ask to be lifted onto the slide.

You saw great progress and now complete new assessments and begin the cycle of assess, plan, do, review again to continue to further Aaron's development.

Supporting the four broad areas of need

When we consider how inclusive our practice is, we must be confident that what we are providing supports a range of children. We often find it clearer and more beneficial for children to focus on their needs rather than a diagnosis. For example, a child who faces challenges communicating has a communication need whether this is due to Global Development Delay, being neurodivergent, or medical needs from birth. The diagnosis or label won't impact the provision you set out to support communication needs. Whilst it is important to know and understand the different diagnoses children will have, it will not change your ability to promote inclusion. The SEND Code of Practice outlines the four broad areas of need as:

Communication and Interaction: Where children have challenges communicating with others, this may be challenges in expressing what they want, understanding what is being said to them, or where they do not understand or use social rules of communication.

Cognition and Learning: Where children may appear to learn at a slower pace than their peers, these may be moderate or severe learning difficulties (MLD/SLD) or profound and multiple learning difficulties (PMLD) where children may require support in all areas of the curriculum.

Social, Emotional and Mental Health: Where children may display a range of behaviours that reflect a variety of underlying mental health difficulties.

Sensory and/or Physical Needs: Where children may have a physical disability that impacts their mobility, vision, hearing or a multi-sensory impairment and adaptations are required to enable them to access their learning.

Recognising what these different needs look like in the early years is key to providing effective support for children. For more information on identifying and assessing children's needs, read "Chapter 4: Monitoring and assessment".

Case study: inclusive practice fundamentals in practice

Welcome to Dingley's Promise Gloucester!

Our team works together to create an environment inclusive to all, utilising resources and approaches to ensure that children of all needs are able to access a range of opportunities to promote their learning and development.

Within our centre, we promote a strong key person approach, enabling each child to have an adult attuned to their individual needs and communication methods. By focusing on these strong relationships, we are able to nurture children's wellbeing and promote a calm environment in which children can access learning at their own pace. The key person works with the SENCO, parents, and other professionals involved to ensure they are all providing consistent support that meets the child's needs and is centred around the child's strengths and interests.

For all children, we introduce communication boards which enable access to a range of communication methods, giving children the opportunity to communicate their key needs from the moment they start with us. Having multiple methods of communication allows children to select the method that works for them, whether this is physical objects, photographs, or symbols. These objects are at child-accessible heights, so that children can touch and move them to share their wants and needs with those around them. The impact of this communication board has led to an increase in positive communication interactions between children and the adults supporting them. It has enabled us to reduce their frustration as they can readily express their needs, such as using the grass object/photograph to indicate when they would like to be outdoors. It also enables team members to clearly indicate instructions and the next steps of the daily routine, such as having a nappy symbol readily available to prepare their key child to go to the bathroom to get their nappy changed.

Our educators have all received inclusion training and regularly reflect on their practice to ensure it is right for the children they are currently supporting. Every educator believes in the importance of opportunity and seek to adapt and adjust experiences so that every child will be able to access it in a way that is meaningful to them. When exploring mark making to encourage the development of gross and fine motor skills, we presented the same core experience in three different ways.

Provocation 1: Large paper is laid out on the floor with an array of brushes, sponges and mark-making tools and a variety of paints and crayons. Copies of Kandinsky's artwork are visible, alongside extracts from "The Noisy Paintbox" musical instruments and instrumental music playing. Educators can encourage children to use their whole body to make marks in different sizes, responding to music and creating freely. They should model interacting with resources themselves, joining this free painting provocation, using language to model new vocabulary e.g. "happy", "brush" and "sounds". Mark-making resources should be available for children who perhaps prefer not to get their hands messy; this way children are still included in the experience and can engage in a way that is comfortable for them. If educators repeat this provocation over a number of sessions as the child grows in confidence, they may choose to use their hands in the future and express themselves freely.

Provocation 2: The same resources as arrangement one should be available, this time with paper hung vertically on an easel in a quieter area, alongside the large-scale painting provocation. Children can benefit from developing gross motor skills making vertical marks and movements alongside the larger group activity. This will support children who engage in solitary or parallel play and prefer to interact in their own ways alongside their peers. Educators may decide to add cars to this provocation, identifying that a child in the cohort is interested in vehicles and moving wheels and using this interest to engage them in the curriculum activity.

Provocation 3: The same resources can be set up for an individual approach. When considering accessibility, children who may be using standing aids and equipment can engage in this provocation, by educators providing smaller paper on their personal tray space and modelling interaction with mark making, sounds, and movements in the same way. Including them within the creative space and modelling body motions and movements, to encourage them to engage with the sensory stimuli of music and painting.

During the experience, educators wore visual lanyards to communicate what was available to the children; they also utilised visuals to reflect the emotions mentioned within the story. There were a range of different heights and surfaces to meet the needs of all children, including a chalkboard for vertical painting to encourage cross-body painting and develop gross motor skills, as shown in Figure 1.2. Educators encouraged children to interact in a way that is comfortable for them, adding resources based on children's interests such as cars to motivate and engage.

Strategies to support and engage children with different needs

Throughout this book, we will make reference to a range of simple strategies that can be applied in a range of scenarios to support a variety of children within your provision and to promote inclusion within your practice. The purpose of these strategies is to address the resources provided and actions of educators, so that we are providing a space in which the child can engage and have their needs met.

Here is a glossary of strategies and where to find more detail throughout this book:

Introduction to inclusive practice 11

Figure 1.2 Adapting a provocation to meet a variety of needs

Communication and interaction	Cognition and learning
Visual timetable (pages 61, 103, 113)	Making adaptions to meet need (pages 2, 6, 125)
Clearly labelled environment – photographs or symbols (pages 108-109)	Chunking information or breakdown of tasks (pages 46, 152)
Clear repetition and modelling language (pages 57, 58, 62, 63, 66, 108)	Repetitive activities (pages 57, 63, 108)
Communication boards (also referred to as language aided boards) (pages 46, 64, 65)	Role play (pages 60, 111)
Match +1 (page 65)	Structured/unstructured play (pages 63, 113)
Objects of reference (pages 59, 61, 64)	Mark making both indoors and outdoors (pages 10, 111)
Choice boards (page 59)	Scaffolding learning (page 152)
Sound buttons (pages 27, 65)	Using multi-sensory approaches to (page 58)
Makaton (pages 59, 61)	
Role play (pages 60, 111)	
Sand timers (page 129)	
Educators wearing lanyards with visuals (pages 6, 10)	

Social, emotional and mental health	Physical and/or sensory
Calm spaces within the environment (page 109)	Opportunities for movement (page 107, 111)
Calm box (pages 35, 109, 152)	Accessible walkways and furniture (enabling walkers/wheelchairs/other mobility equipment) this should be considered both indoors and out (page 111)
Low arousal approach (page 109)	Experiences across different heights (page 111)
Mindful and Calming techniques for example deep breathing, massage (page 152)	Consideration of environmental stimuli (page 108)
Containment approaches: touch/mirroring/movement/voice (page 66)	Sensory - calm space (page 109)
Social stories (pages 130, 150)	Sensory toys and regulation resources (page 128)
Labelling emotions (page 103)	
Modelling your own emotions and how to respond to those (page 103)	Equipment and resources that are developmentally appropriate e.g. 'squeezy' scissors/left-handed scissors; mark-making tools that can be gripped/manipulated/used according to physical needs (page 139)
Consistency of routine and boundaries (pages 113, 130, 134, 142)	Using specialist equipment which enables them to access the environment or resources. (page 111)
Observations of attachment styles as part of transition, as this will indicate how to build strong and positive relationships, especially with a key person (pages 32, 34, 35)	Reasonable adjustments (page 4)
Stories and use of puppets/characters (page 103)	
Books which explore emotions (page 151)	
Transitional object/transition book (page 35, 141)	

Reflection time

Ask yourself or your team the following questions:

Consider the support you provide to children in your provision. How do you provide universal, targeted and specialist support based on children's individual needs?

Do you know where to find and understand the Ordinarily Available Provision expected within your local authority?

How does your provision readily meet the needs of children with different needs? (Consider the four broad areas of need)

How do you ensure the voice of the family is included in the assess, plan, do, review cycle?

References and further reading

Department for Education (2015) Special Educational Needs and Disability Code of Practice: 0 to 25 Years [Available at: https://www.gov.uk/government/publications/send-code-of-practice-0-to-25].
Equality Act (2010) [Available at: https://www.legislation.gov.uk/ukpga/2010/15/section/20].

2
Leadership and management of inclusion

Meggie Fisher and Lee Friend

> **KEY DEFINITIONS**
>
> Leadership: Leading a group of people, demonstrating positive influence and guidance to achieve a common goal.
> Management: Organising and controlling the resources available to you, including people, to meet specific outcomes.
> Vision: To have a clear image, idea or understanding of something that may not be immediately present, but is a future possibility.
> Curriculum: A holistic and ambitious plan of what you want children to learn across the seven areas of learning in the Early Years Foundation Stage (EYFS).
> Pedagogy: The approach you take to teach children – the way you will deliver the curriculum to them.

Introduction

The leadership and management of inclusion are pivotal to the success of creating an inclusive provision. As managers, it is key that we understand the systems and procedures in place to aid our inclusive practice and promote effective inclusion. As leaders, we must ensure we are modelling, inspiring and living the inclusive ethos we want to see so that our team, families and children join us in promoting inclusion. We know that it is important to promote inclusivity within our settings and to share this as part of our vision and values. However, it is also key to be able to identify how inclusive your team is. The SEND Code of Practice makes it clear that inclusion is a duty – something that providers often value but can sometimes get lost when trying to run a business and make ends meet. We need to identify how being inclusive can benefit a business and focus on those strategies so that child, family and business benefit. This chapter will explore how to build your vision, build your awareness of the population and market within your local area and how to instil inclusive values across your curriculum and pedagogical approach.

Vision

When developing your vision as a team, a great place to start is to consider why you do what you do. Asking yourself and your team key questions about why you all work in childcare and why you value inclusion, can help you build the basis of your vision for your setting. Once you have established "why" you can move on to what, how and who and piece together the important details of your setting vision. Involving your team members in this process will enable them to understand how inclusion is part of their daily roles and responsibilities and what part they play in achieving this inclusive vision.

As a leader, it is crucial that you live your vision every day. You might say that the setting is going to be open to all children, but if a child with SEND applies to join and you turn them away saying there is a more inclusive setting down the road, then this is what your teams will remember.

Questions to consider when developing your settings vision:

- What is our purpose?
- What kind of organisation do we wish to be?
- What impact do we want to have on the children in our care?
- What are our values and how does our vision reflect them?

Business planning for inclusion

A business plan helps to create a set of actions you are going to take to achieve your aims and objectives. When thinking about your business plan, understanding how inclusion and SEND play a part in this is crucial.

Figure 2.1 Children's rubber boots are hung on a wooden fence

Market research of your area

Understanding the supply and demand within the area in which you are operating and the wider local area, can help you ensure that your intended vision and objectives are realistic and achievable. All local authorities are required to publish a Childcare Sufficiency Assessment (CSA) as part of their Sufficiency Duties under the Childcare Act 2006. These documents should be available online and can be utilised as a starting point to understanding childcare in your area. A CSA should not only tell you about the population of children but how many are likely to have SEND. They should also predict demand for provision and the places available (supply locally) in order to identify gaps. There will always be a percentage of children with SEND in any population, so factoring this in will be key. In general, across the country we would expect to see around 10% of children in the early years having SEND needs. If we want to live in inclusive, diverse communities (and society), our mainstream settings will reflect the local population we are aiming to serve.

As well as looking at the available data, it is vital that you speak to families about their needs. Engaging in conversation, as well as regular parent surveys, can help you understand family priorities, desired sessions, awareness of funding entitlements, working positions, and other family dynamics which may impact their uptake of childcare.

Understanding the local SEND population

Knowing how many children with SEND are expected in your local population can significantly aid your planning. You can ask your local authority for this figure or find it in your local Childcare Sufficiency Assessment document. Once you know the percentage of children expected in the early years, you can compare it to the percentage of children with SEND in your setting. If your setting has significantly fewer or significantly more children with SEND than expected, it may be worth considering the potential reasons why.

If your setting has fewer children with SEND than the local average, it could indicate several issues:

- **Identification Support:** Your team may need support identifying potential SEND.
- **Reputation:** Unfortunately, your setting may have a reputation for not being inclusive, so families may not choose to apply to you.
- **Welcoming Environment:** Your setting might not appear welcoming and inclusive, causing some families who contact you to choose other settings.
- **Local Demographics:** There may be fewer children with SEND in your area.
- **Turning Away Children:** In some cases, settings themselves are actively turning away children with SEND despite equality law. Research from the Early Years Alliance found that 28% of settings reported doing this.

Reasons for higher SEND enrolment

Alternatively, if your setting has more children with SEND than the local average, it could highlight:

- **Strong Reputation:** You may have a strong reputation for being inclusive and supporting SEND families, so other organisations refer to you, and families are actively choosing you.
- **Local Demographics:** There may be a disproportionate number of children with SEND in your area, possibly due to being based in a more deprived area, as research demonstrates the correlation between poverty and SEND.
- **Proximity to Medical Facilities:** Being near a children's hospital could increase the likelihood that local children requiring medical care attend your setting.

Your business planning process needs to hold the most vulnerable children at its heart, whilst thinking about the bigger picture in terms of income, to support the highest quality inclusive provision possible. Taking into consideration the needs and wants of your families and researching your local funding streams alongside the demand, will enable you to welcome and celebrate all children, with the peace of mind that you remain financially sustainable and true to your vision and values.

Calculating your potential income

To enable your setting to run you need to ensure that your income at least balances with your outgoings, so it is important to plan for all your anticipated revenue streams as well as your regular costs, so that you can understand what impact any alterations you may make to your service will have on your future sustainability. When considering your income you should establish all direct income streams (fees for provision and services, and nursery education funding). You can then use this to map your operational model of delivery and illustrate what your potential income could be from your fees and NE funding. Remember to consider your average occupancy here, taking into account quiet times of the day, week, term and year when you will not be as full as others. Being realistic about your occupancy will help you to ensure you operate with a surplus as opposed to a deficit.

You should also be aware of indirect income streams which help parents and carers reduce the cost of childcare, e.g. Tax-Free Childcare, Universal Credit, Working Tax Credit, Care to Learn etc.. These avenues can make childcare more accessible to parents and so increase your occupancy and viability.

There are also local and national grants which you and your setting may be able to apply for and opportunities to fundraise and generous "in kind" support from volunteers and community supporters.

Are you familiar enough with the specific funding and support available for inclusion?

Disability Access Fund (DAF)	For supporting reasonable adjustments to provision. This is paid annually for every child who has Disability Living Allowance (DLA). It is the family's responsibility to apply for DLA – something that many families are not ready or confident to do. If you can support the family with this (assuming they are happy to do so), you will get access to this funding.

(Continued)

18 *Early years inclusive practice for children with SEND*

Inclusion Fund to Support Emerging Needs	There are a wide range of processes to apply for this funding across the country. Some LAs are moving to a focus on reporting and impact of the funding rather than detailed application processes, whilst others are still focused on detailed applications and panels to allocate the funds. If you have a child whose needs are emerging, then this will help you to fund anything that would not normally be available under the "Ordinarily Available Provision" document for your area. Many local authorities prefer to fund enhanced ratios due to the negative impacts on children of having a one-to-one adult with them at all times, so this is something to consider.
The High Needs Block (HNB)	Designed to fund support for children with more complex needs in the early years. If the child you are supporting has high or complex needs, then they are likely to have an EHCP or be on the pathway to securing an EHCP. Again, this varies in local authority areas, but for these children you should talk to your local authority about funding to support their needs through the HNB.
Higher Rate Tax-Free Childcare for Working Parents	Up to £4000 per year towards childcare costs for children with a disability.
Universal Credit	
Direct Payments	Or personal budgets.
Disability Living Allowance	Can also be used towards childcare costs.
Flexible Working	Parents have the right to request flexible working if they have a disabled child.

Working collaboratively across services

Leading an inclusive provision requires strong leadership that can drive meaningful inclusive practices, ensuring every child can access their early years education. When inclusion is close to your heart, it's essential to understand that being an inclusive setting is not a silo in which you sit alone. The strength of inclusion comes from working in collaboration with other services available in your area; this includes the local authority, health services, other provisions and schools. You can work with your local authority team to understand what additional support, funding, and training are available. Liaise with health professionals to understand the support available in your area, navigate long wait times for children's referrals and embed good practices within your team. Sharing your concerns and challenges with a solution-focused mindset and supporting others by spreading good inclusive practice, ultimately increases spaces available in your area for children with Special Educational Needs and Disabilities (SEND) and reduces pressures on settings considered to have a strong SEND reputation.

Working with other local settings to share best practice and knowledge is beneficial for developing effective inclusive practices across all early years provisions. You can create

Leadership and management of inclusion 19

links by engaging with or establishing regular networking meetings within your area; these can even involve members of the local authority early years/SEND/inclusion teams. Meetings can offer opportunities for collaboration and planning as shown in Figure 2.2. Where you are able to, this could also take the form of visits to observe inclusive practice, or through phone or email support when other settings have concerns or challenges. This support network can also benefit your relationships with local schools, modelling how inclusive practice works well in your setting and providing opportunities for them to see how they can continue to provide inclusion for children transitioning into their next stage of education. The transition process for children with SEND can be overwhelming and lacking in strong information sharing. By developing these relationships early, you can understand the schools' expectations and support the schools to be prepared to meet the needs of their new children. For more information on transitions, see "Chapter 11: Transitions for children with SEND."

Keeping your local authority informed if you have a high percentage of children with SEND is crucial. This communication helps them understand which settings are delivering well and could lead to more support for your setting or assistance for other settings to admit children with SEND. Your local authority should be your ally, committed to helping every child access early years education, so regular sharing of information and concerns is valuable.

As they seek to embed high-quality provision and improve sufficiency for children with SEND, many local authorities hold forums, committee meetings, or other engagement groups to gather evidence and feedback from providers and services. Engaging with these meetings will strengthen your connections with other services, support your own understanding of how your roles integrate, and enable you to share your voice to improve support services for children in your area.

Figure 2.2 Photograph of planning board, exploring key areas of the curriculum and how they can be enhanced to support children's specific needs

Leading an inclusive provision is a multifaceted responsibility that requires strong leadership, collaboration with local authorities, health services and other provisions and schools, and a commitment to understanding and addressing the needs of children with SEND. By fostering an inclusive environment, sharing best practices, and maintaining open communication with all who support children with SEND, settings can ensure that every child has access to quality early years education. This approach not only benefits the children and their families but also strengthens the overall provision of early years education in the community.

Inclusive curriculum

Providing or creating a curriculum that promotes inclusion, will support how effectively your team are able to promote inclusive practice every day. When thinking about what makes your curriculum inclusive, you should consider the following:

1. Use available resources and guidance to plan the content of your own curriculum; EYFS statutory framework, non-statutory guidance documents (Development Matters, Birth to Five), Dingley's Promise early years SEND curriculum; you could also consider the theorists that influence best practice.
2. Research and ensure you have a sound understanding of your legal duties in relation to both the EYFS and the SEND code of practice to ensure all children are included within provision planning.
3. Recognise where policy changes may be needed within your provision, so that positive changes can be implemented.
4. Prioritise staff training, mentoring and one-to-ones – educators may need additional support during a period of change.
5. Consider the individual needs of all children that attend your provision; you will want to determine how they are learning and what you would like them to learn whilst they are in attendance.
6. Think about the reasonable adjustments your provision can and will make to become inclusive and set the expectation with the whole team. It can help to identify when specialist help might assist children with specific needs, e.g. Occupational Therapists providing children with equipment so they can progress and engage more positively in the environment.
7. Identify your expectations for all children that attend your provision and ensure your curriculum is ambitious and doesn't limit children's opportunities.
8. Ensure your curriculum is holistic and that it considers individual identity and sense of belonging within children's local community.
9. Plan and provide provocations, play and real-life experiences that help children learn what you want them to learn.
10. Review and reflect on the changes made – observe and assess the impact of your curriculum on children's wellbeing, learning and development. Plan time to effectively review its implementation and educators' understanding. Adapt and make continuous

improvements until you are fully satisfied with your curriculum and educators can implement it confidently and effectively.

Once you have carefully considered what you want children to learn, it is also important to consider your pedagogy or how you are going to teach children. Reflecting on different pedagogical approaches can support the development of you and your team's practice and ensure you are upholding the same values of inclusion.

Pedagogical influences on inclusive practice

As professionals looking to constantly improve provision, it is important to acknowledge different approaches and reflect on how appropriate they are in supporting children's development and learning and how effectively they encourage us to develop inclusion. Knowing and understanding influences on your practice will support you in guiding and supporting your team to deliver your curriculum as anticipated.

Theorists and approaches, both new and old, discuss the importance of understanding the unique child, giving each child the opportunity to have their voice and being adaptive to the needs of each individual. Influence can be taken from many pedagogical ideas to develop your inclusive practice.

The Reggio Emilia approach puts children at the centre of their learning. The hundred languages give the child the capacity to communicate through a variety of means, such as gestures, glances, emotion, dance, music and sculpture amongst many others, making it extremely expressive with an enormous capacity for sharing feelings and emotions. It observes and listens to children's needs, valuing the multitude of ways children can communicate and share their voice, views, and opinions.

The Mosaic approach makes children's voices visible and heard in the adult community, using and integrating visual and verbal tools such as observations, dialogue, manipulation of objects, photographs, and drawings. This approach allows children to physically see and explore the findings from their own learning themselves. This can be done by using diverse modes such as videos, pictures, plants, smells and textures from real materials, often within the outdoor environment. Children can participate as documenters, photographers, initiators, and commentators, taking the lead and an active role in which ideas, people, places, and objects are given significance.

The Montessori approach is adaptive to the needs of each child, with educators playing a crucial role in providing the right materials for children to explore at the right point in their development. It promotes a well-prepared environment in which children have freedom of choice and movement as they develop independence, autonomy and a positive sense of self and accomplishment.

The Stiener-Waldolf approach observes growth and development as three phases: 0-7 years, 7-14 years and 14-21 years. A rounded development in one phase is believed to be essential for the child to move on to the next phase. It focuses on imaginative and holistic methods to support children in reaching their full potential as creative, intelligent and well-rounded human beings. Steiner nurseries cater for children in mixed age and ability classes and also place value on engaging with families through playgroups.

Te Whāriki is a child-centred curriculum adopted within early childhood education in New Zealand. This approach has a strong focus on well-being and learning age-appropriate content, tolerance and respect for cultural values and diversity. Te Whāriki prepares children for school by teaching and building resilience and risk-taking, rather than focusing on their literacy and numeracy developmental milestones. Educators assess children using a combination of narratives or learning stories, careful observations, and reflective practice to enhance children's development and learning opportunities. This curriculum is based on four principles; these include:

Empowerment: The early childhood curriculum empowers the child to learn and grow.
Holistic Development: Early childhood curriculum reflects the holistic way children learn and grow.
Family and Community: The wider world of family and community is an integral part of the early childhood curriculum.
Relationships: Children learn through responsive and reciprocal relationships with people, places and things.

Hygge is a Danish word which has no literal translation to English; however, it refers to the feeling of warmth and focuses on joy, togetherness and living in the moment. This concept has been embedded within Danish early education and is becoming increasingly popular throughout the world and in other pedagogical approaches to early childhood education. The hygge approach adopts ten core elements within early years settings, including:

- **Atmosphere:** Creating a warm, calm and homely setting.
- **Presence:** Focus on what they are doing and feeling right here, right now.
- **Pleasure:** Activities that are fun and promote happiness and wellbeing.
- **Equality:** Sharing and respect for others.
- **Togetherness:** Spending quality time together and forming strong friendships.
- **Gratitude:** Time to reflect and discuss what they are grateful for.
- **Harmony:** Less focus on competitiveness and instead enjoying playing together.
- **Truce:** Learning to play fairly and manage conflict.
- **Comfort:** A comfortable, cosy environment.
- **Shelter:** Space to relax or read alone.

Conclusion

As a leader within early years, it is vital that you lead by example, engage with other professionals and services, and develop your team to deliver strong inclusive practice. Your influence will impact your team and their perception of inclusion, as well as the families who attend your setting.

When making decisions about offering a place to a child, always consider your legal and moral duties to children and their families. As the first educational setting a family may contact, your decision will significantly impact them and their perception of the future for their child. If a family is told that the setting cannot meet their child's needs, they may lose trust in the mainstream education system's ability to support their child effectively. This could result in the child staying at home until school starts, missing out on critical early intervention and support opportunities.

Developing an inclusive approach as part of your typical delivery increases opportunities for children with SEND, embeds support for those children from other services, and increases the likelihood of successful transitions to school. What we do in the early years matters.

Reflection time

Do you know your local SEND population? Review your area's Child Sufficiency Assessment to determine what possible proportion of children you should expect to have SEND in your setting.

Ask your team what your nursery vision is. Do they share the same vision as you, and are they confident in what role they play in achieving this?

Is your curriculum accessible to all children? How do you know children are learning what you set out to teach?

References and further reading

Clark, A. & Moss, P. (2011) *Listening to Young Children: The Mosaic Approach*. London: NCB.
Department for Education (2021) *Development Matters: Non-statutory Curriculum Guidance for the Early Years Foundation Stage*. [Available at: https://assets.publishing.service.gov.uk/media/64e6002a20ae890014f26cbc/DfE_Development_Matters_Report_Sep2023.pdf].
Department for Education (2024) *Statutory Framework for Group and School-based Providers* [Available at: https://www.gov.uk/government/publications/early-years-foundation-stage-framework--2].
Department for Education (2024) *Statutory Framework for Childminders*. [Available at: https://www.gov.uk/government/publications/early-years-foundation-stage-framework--2].
Dingley's Promise (2024) "Business Planning for Inclusion." *Childcare Works* [Available at: https://childcareworks.org.uk/dingleys-promise-business-planning-for-inclusion-slides-with-audio/].
Early Years Coalition. (2021). *Birth to 5 Matters: Non-statutory Guidance for the Early Years Foundation Stage*. St Albans: Early Education [Available at https://birthto5matters.org.uk/wp-content/uploads/2021/04/Birthto5Matters-download.pdf].
Grenier, J. & Vollans, C. (2023) *Putting the EYFS Curriculum into Practice*. London: Sage.
https://www.reggiochildren.it/en/reggio-emilia-approach/.
https://tewhariki.tahurangi.education.govt.nz/te-whariki/our-curriculum/about-our-curriculum/5637149826.c.
Munson, S. (updated 2025) *Hygge Nurseries: Practising Hygge in Early Years* [Available at: https://www.daynurseries.co.uk/advice/hygge-nurseries-practising-hygge-in-early-years].
Pound, L. (2011) *Influencing Ealy Childhood Education: Key Figures, Philosophies and Ideas*. Berkshire: Open University Press.

3
Early identification

Louise White

> **KEY DEFINITIONS**
>
> Early identification: The recognition of the need for support for a child to access their learning at the earliest opportunity.
> Areas of need: The four broad areas of need as defined by the SEND Code of Practice. An area of learning and development where a child may require a different approach, adaptation of resources or additional support to enable them to make progress.
> Diagnosis: The identification of an illness or developmental difference through examination by a health professional.

Introduction

The importance of early identification of Special Educational Needs and Disabilities (SEND) cannot be overstated. It plays a crucial role in providing children with the appropriate support that is vital for their development and long-term outcomes. Early identification ensures that support is put in place as soon as possible, and research consistently shows that the earlier a need is recognised, the better the chances for effective support, leading to improved long-term outcomes and a positive life-long impact.

As the Department for Education (DfE) highlights within the SEND Code of Practice (2015), "Identifying need at the earliest point, and then making effective provision, improves long-term outcomes for children". This resonates deeply in settings where educators must be proactive in detecting SEND, so children can fully access the environment and curriculum and as a result, continue to make progress with their learning and development. This proactive approach significantly benefits both the child and the family, helping to avoid secondary issues such as frustration, delayed academic progress and emotional struggles.

Benefits of early identification

Early identification enables the implementation of targeted support tailored to a child's unique needs. For example, early identification of speech delays can lead to educators immediately responding with additional communication strategies such as introducing objects of reference or focusing on key Makaton signs. Where support is implemented immediately, the child can start to make progress with their communication, reducing the long-term impact on learning and development. If this early intervention does not support the child in making significant or expected progress with their communication, referrals to services such as speech and language therapy can be made, as adequate evidence of the child's strengths and needs will have been gathered, so that additional specialist support can be more targeted and effective. Through early identification, children are more likely to reach their full potential and be given the best start, reducing other difficulties such as behavioural challenges or low self-esteem.

This early support benefits families too. It enables them to gain greater awareness and understanding of their child's needs and helps them to provide the right support for their child at home. It gives them time to build trusting relationships with key professionals and engage with the services they have to offer, to enhance the support being provided to their child. A key benefit is that it can reduce family stress and frustration that might be experienced from a delay in accessing support and interventions. When families are informed early, they are better positioned to build resilience and provide consistent support at home and in educational settings. For example, children experiencing frustration as a result of unmet needs may display behaviours that those around them find challenging. Identifying this early can prepare parents and carers with strategies to support their child in the moment and arm them with ways to support themselves to remain regulated when their child isn't, so that challenges do not escalate and they are able to confidently support their child in the moment.

Recognising areas of need early also benefits educators, by encouraging them to regularly reflect on their environment and practice to ensure they are adaptive with their teaching to meet the child's needs. Children whose needs are being met are less likely to experience stress responses and, as a result, display behaviour that challenges those around them.

Recognising needs early also reduces the potential for children to 'fall through the cracks'. As all children learn and develop at different rates, there may be children who only require short periods of support for a specific need or children who may have emerging needs that can be met more easily at this early point than if they were left to wait and see how their development goes. Recognising and beginning to discuss children's needs with their parents and carers and implementing early support strategies, ensures that attention is being paid to their needs and that their support journey has started.

Regular discussions about child development and training on special educational needs and disabilities enable educators to become more skilled, supporting them to identify needs early. This builds their confidence and the confidence of their team, as they are all working to support and include children in their practice.

26 *Early years inclusive practice for children with SEND*

Not only is early identification better for the life outcomes of the child, but the earlier the action, the less it is likely to cost the education system, enabling funding to go further and reach more children. Where support has been implemented effectively, children with SEND are more able to access a mainstream environment, whether this is in the early years or as they move into school. Accessing mainstream provision with the right support in place costs less than accessing specialist provision and frees up specialist places for those that need them. There are also more mainstream places available to children than specialist, therefore more children are able to take up their entitlement.

Case study: how early identification has enabled Child P to access support and make good progress with her development

At aged 18 months, Child P's mother was concerned that she was not developing in the same way as her older siblings had previously. After discussion with a medical professional, P was sent for genetic testing where anomalies were found, and an initial diagnosis of Spinocerebellar Ataxia 18 was made. However, with further tests, they were unwilling to commit to this diagnosis, and she now has the diagnosis of Syndrome Without A Name (SWAN) – as further monitoring is needed to make a more concrete diagnosis. P has hyper-reflexia in her lower limbs and overactive body reflexes. P initially needed support to walk unaided and to ensure her safety. P was also non-verbal, and her parents were anxious about her settling and her progress. It was recommended that P attended Dingley's Promise to receive early intervention and support to help progress her learning and development.

After her initial settling visits at Dingley's Promise, we were able to identify her interests and develop support through these. For example, she loved music and singing, and we were able to develop positive relationships through this and, in turn, increase her interaction skills and introduce and model different communication strategies.

Figure 3.1 Child exploring musical sensory basket

Implementation of support

We role-modelled and played alongside P with activities that she enjoyed, such as sensory play, using the cause-and-effect toys, music and dancing and looking at books. We used Makaton and role-modelled speech using reduced language, along with visuals or objects of reference to support P's understanding of the activity and routines. We used visuals to offer choices so P could voice her preference by pointing to what she wanted.

We used recorded voice output buttons so that P could use them independently to hear different words relating to an activity. We also used large puzzle boards with a different sound behind each door so that P could hear animal noises and their names. We used a now and next board so that P could be prepared for what activity was coming next.

Impact of support

P's confidence grew very quickly, and she demonstrated an interest in many activities and toys. She was able to explore and access activities and play independently and also participate in adult-led activities such as sensory play, mark making, painting and role-play. By hearing reduced language and watching the adult role-modelling, this developed P's understanding so that she felt confident trying things independently. Through the support and gradual build-up of P's attention and listening, she was able to sit independently and her attention and listening skills improved so that she could benefit from listening to sensory stories and looking at books with her key person.

By using reduced language alongside visuals and objects of reference, this developed P's understanding of the routine and she looked for visual clues such as the sand timer or the music on the tablet. P's speech rapidly developed over the year and she started using many single words before starting to put two words together.

P started at a mainstream nursery doing split provision with us. She then went on to mainstream school with support full time and is doing extremely well (Figure 3.1).

Engaging families and overcoming barriers

While the benefits of early identification are clear, educators need to be aware of potential barriers families might face and understand ways to navigate and support parents through these.

Some may not recognise the typical developmental milestones or the importance of early interventions. Educators must engage families effectively, providing clear information and resources to empower them.

Moreover, cultural differences and differing perspectives on SEND can shape how families perceive developmental concerns. It is important for educators to approach these discussions with empathy and respect, ensuring that the family feels supported and understood.

At times it may be that specialist services may be limited or there could be long waiting lists for services, and having educators be that advocate for children and families is a key part of the role to ensure they can access the appropriate support.

There are many different ways in which you can work with parents and carers to develop positive relationships that support the early identification of need process, such as:

- Offering information sessions that parents can engage with and build on skills and knowledge to best support the family/child within the home environment. These are most beneficial when they cover topics that are particularly relevant to your families, note down the common questions families ask and plan your session around these or ask parents what they'd like to know more about.
- Meeting within the setting to show progress and work collaboratively to agree targets for both home and setting. Ensure you are offering tailored strategies for use in the home so that they are able to actively support their child and extend their learning.
- Building those fundamental relationships by meeting with families to learn from them about their child's strengths and difficulties to support partnership working.
- Gathering feedback and suggestions, sharing cultural and personal experiences that can enhance the curriculum and activities on offer.
- Offering stay-and-play sessions that are for the family, with educators on hand to role-model play skills and support in the moment.

Parent engagement bridges the gap between home and setting and can make the child feel supported in both environments.

Early identification: from pregnancy to preschool

Early identification begins long before a child enters formal education. It may start in pre-natal care through medical or genetic testing, with the recognition of potential conditions or challenges. Early identification at this stage allows parents to connect with relevant support networks, such as health visitors or specialised groups, to prepare for the needs their child may have.

After birth, health check-ups like the newborn hearing test, regular developmental reviews and observations by health visitors continue the identification process. When a child's needs are recognised early, families are better equipped to provide consistent support at home, and they become more open to collaborating with other professionals who can support their child. This process also normalises discussions about developmental differences, reducing the stigma that sometimes surrounds SEND.

Not all children will have their needs recognised prior to starting within an early years provision, so it is also key that early years educators are skilled and confident in early identification. Educators play a key role in identifying and supporting children with SEND. Their observations and reflective practices help build a deeper understanding of each child's individual needs. Consistently assessing a child's progress through formative and summative assessments provides educators with the data they need to make informed decisions about how best to support each child.

The role of educators in early identification

Early recognition of SEND enables educators to make adaptations to the learning environment that ensures inclusivity and access to the curriculum. Educators who are confident in their learning environment and how it supports inclusion are prepared and able to make adaptations and adjustments in the moment as needed for each child. For example, an environment prepared to support a range of communication needs would have strategies such as visual aids readily available at the point of identification to begin implementing support. This eases potential challenges and can reduce frustrations that impact the child and the setting.

Educators can engage in the early identification process and refine their observations and reflective skills to benefit all children as when the educators become more attuned to individual needs and respond with strategies that support the child better.

Even with no formal diagnosis, educators must adopt an inclusive approach that supports all children, regardless of their developmental stage. They should strive to create a place that celebrates diversity and can accommodate a range of learning styles and needs, such as providing a variety of learning opportunities that are tailored to a child's individual strengths and interests. It is important that there is a consistent approach to observing and assessing children's development and to identifying any emerging needs across the whole team, so that all children receive the same timely identification and support they need. Educators should work closely with the family and other professionals to create consistent strategies that support this and stay informed about SEND through continued professional development.

The DfE Early Years SEND Assessment Toolkit, developed by Dingley's Promise, is an excellent resource for educators, offering a structured approach to identifying and supporting children with SEND. The toolkit allows educators to evaluate a child's developmental needs systematically, with practical tools and guidance that support a strengths-based, child-centred approach. This enables educators to assess needs early, facilitating timely intervention (Figure 3.2).

For more information on assessment, see "Chapter 4: Monitoring and assessment".

Is it always SEND?

While SEND is a primary focus for many children, it is essential to consider other factors that might mimic or intersect with SEND, such as English as an Additional Language (EAL), attachment issues, adverse childhood experiences or major life events. It is essential that we evaluate whether these challenges arise from the circumstances of life rather than SEND, and we can then tailor the response accordingly.

Supporting children and their families who speak English as an additional language

Children with EAL may appear to have learning challenges or communication difficulties that are actually due to language barriers. They may be reluctant to engage or have difficulty following instructions, which could be mistaken for developmental delays.

Figure 3.2 Educators observing physical progress in practice

Figures tell us that there are almost 230,000 children in schools in England who speak or are thought to speak a language other than English who also have SEND (DfE, 2023). It is vital, therefore, that those children are identified as early as possible and receive targeted and integrated support that addresses both their linguistic challenges and their specific learning needs.

Numbers of children who are learning English as an additional language are increasing, but it's vital that we understand that children who may not be achieving expected progress in specific areas of learning due to learning English as an additional language is not the same as having SEND. For example, a child who is learning initial sounds or phrases in English may find it challenging and take time to grasp the concepts, but they need to be given time to understand what is being taught alongside translating it into their home language to ensure they develop a secure understanding.

It is essential that you do not make assumptions when supporting your EAL children. Children in the early stages of English language acquisition should not be identified as having learning difficulties. In addition, slow academic progress should not be assumed to be because of their additional language needs.

When it comes to supporting children and families who speak English as an additional language with (or without) SEND, there is lots that can be done by early years educators to have a positive impact on children and families.

It is important that you value and respect children's home language and include these in children's early education.

- You may wish to consider how you can include children's home languages with purpose in your setting; for example, including home languages on room signs or resource labelling.
- You may ask families to provide phonetically spelt words in their home language to use alongside your routine, e.g. "snack", "nappy", "garden" so that you can support children's transitions in their home language.
- You may wish to include meaningful resources such as food packaging written in home languages in your home areas.
- Carry out ongoing assessments, including in children's home language, and set targets for language learning in English.
- When sharing information about children's development and assessments with families, consider if these documents can be shared with them in their home language.
- Use apps and advancing technology to support the translation of written formats.
- Encourage family members or friends to attend meetings with parents and/or carers if they are happy to support and translate information.
- Be well prepared for meetings; think about how you can present your worries and concerns in a format that is understood by everyone. For example, can you use photographs or videos to demonstrate what you are saying?

Understanding attachment and how this can affect children with SEND and families

Similarly, attachment issues may lead to behaviours that resemble those seen in children with SEND. Children with insecure attachments may struggle with emotional regulation, social interactions or attention, which can be mistaken for SEND. Educators must recognise the significance of early attachment experiences and adopt appropriate therapeutic strategies to support these children.

There is a wealth of research that shares the importance of developing secure attachments, and we know that having secure attachments with main caregivers has a positive impact on children's development and lives (Bowlby, 1953).

Secure attachments to supportive and caring adults are imperative in the development of a child's emotional well-being. Children need to have their basic needs met to feel cared for and safe. As early years educators, we must be: available, warm, responsive, respectful, comforting and supportive. For a child's brain to create the appropriate pathways that lead to emotional self-regulation, they need to experience numerous effective and varied interactions with a caring adult. Attachment theory highlights the importance of secure attachments between young children and their families. These early bonds form the foundation for a child's emotional and social development. Secure attachments provide children with a sense of safety and predictability, enabling them to explore their environment and engage in learning.

Clear attachment behaviours can be seen in children from an early age. They include crying, reaching out for and moving towards a primary carer. The attachment system kicks in to get basic needs met and attachment behaviours are often seen when a child is in a state of distress, frustration or confusion, and needs help to regulate their emotional response. These behaviours have a goal – for the child to be helped and to feel safe. If the goal is fulfilled by a caring adult, the attachment "alarm system" in the brain is switched off and the child can continue to thrive. However, repeated failed interactions, or a lack of attempted interactions, can cause children to present with continuing attachment problems and anxiety.

As part of our inclusive practice, we should support issues with attachment whether they are trauma-induced, the result of abuse, or are interwoven with a child's SEND. Behaviours that might indicate difficulties with attachment include: hurting other people, staying close to an adult, sudden intense anger, lack of eye contact, lack of stranger danger, excessive crying.

We should always support a child with a bottom-up approach.

Brainstem: Develops first, somatic sensory area.
Limbic: Develops second, attachment, emotional and behavioural regulation area.
Cortical: Develops last, self-esteem and cognition area.

If the needs of the brainstem are not met, the higher functions of the limbic and cortical systems will be impaired. Research shows that adults can meet the child's sensory needs, helping to get the brain back "online" and supporting the connection with adults and regulation for emotional refuelling.

For practical strategies on meeting sensory needs, read Chapter 9: Enabling environments.

Recognising and supporting families with attachment difficulties

Attachment difficulties can manifest in various ways for children; this may include avoidance or other anxious behaviours. These can arise from a range of factors, including parent stress, inconsistent caregiving, or challenges related to SEND.

Recognising signs of attachment issues will require educators and those who provide support to the families (such as family support workers) to be trained in identifying signs of attachment difficulties. This can appear as clinginess, withdrawal or other significant changes to their behaviour. Recognising is the first step in providing appropriate support.

Providing consistent and responsive care can help children develop trust and feel secure, and our key person approach plays a crucial role in providing stability.

Educators support children by encouraging active parental involvement within the setting through activities like stay-and-play sessions, workshops and coffee mornings, which help strengthen the bond between parents and children. They offer guidance on attachment-promoting practices, such as responding to children's needs and maintaining a predictable routine, to enhance the quality of family relationships.

The stronger the family unit, the more likely children are to thrive. Early years educators, through intentional practices and supportive strategies, can contribute significantly to the resilience and well-being of the families we support. The benefits of these efforts extend beyond the early years, laying a foundation for life-long emotional and social well-being in children.

Supporting family resilience and addressing attachment issues are essential ways of promoting child well-being in early years settings. By understanding the dynamics of family resilience and the importance of secure attachments, we can implement strategies that support both children and their families. The result is a stronger, more resilient family unit, which in turn nurtures the development of happy, healthy children. These early interventions and supports have a lasting impact, which is a vital role of early years settings in shaping the future of children and their families.

Attachment difficulties are often associated with families where the parent/carer is unwilling or unable to respond to their child's attachment needs. For example, situations where there is neglect, substance misuse, domestic abuse or parental mental health issues. However, this is not always the case. When a child has SEND, there may also appear to be a lack of a secure attachment between the child and their main caregiver even if other usual influencing factors at home are not present. This can have an impact on the child's behaviour and their emotional regulation.

We must consider general factors that might relate to any family where the child has SEND. They may have a history of hospital care and a lack of stable routines due to illness. They may think adults cause pain/discomfort through medical procedures. There may be confusion over the parent role due to the parents having to fulfil multiple roles including nurse and therapist as well as being a parent. A parent may have their own mental health issues caused by parenting a child who has SEND, or may themselves have poor emotional intelligence and so not understand how to support the emotional intelligence of their child. Lack of sleep may make them less receptive to their child's needs and family relationship breakdown may influence a parent's ability to form an attachment to their child. Poverty can also affect parental capacity to spend time building attachment with their child. Research shows that children with SEND are more likely to be living in poverty and in a single parent family than their peers.

There may also be factors around attachment difficulties relating to the individual child's developmental pattern. They may have difficulties communicating due to speech and language delays or difficulty initiating interactions due to poor mobility. A lack of understanding or appreciation of the benefits of interaction will affect the attachments they make. Sensory processing differences can make a child reluctant to interact with certain people – the touch, sight, smell and sound of another person may be unpleasant or overwhelming to the child. Sleep difficulties or chronic pain/health issues may cause increased levels of tiredness and affect their ability to respond.

Love in your setting is what matters. The revised Development Matters Guidance references love, stating that babies, toddlers and young children thrive when they are loved and well cared for (Department for Education, 2023). To feel safe and thrive, children need to feel loved.

There are a number of ways you can share love and increase children's sense of safety in your setting; Actively listening to children, whether they can communicate verbally or non-verbally, noticing their behaviours, recognising facial expression and body language, following through and acting upon what they are communicating, including them in decisions and using their interests in the environment, giving them your full attention and not talking over them to other educators. Engage them in respectful caregiving, not only acting as their champion but giving them agency and autonomy over what happens during their day, believing that they are competent and capable. When we do all these things to empower children, we are developing their self-efficacy, self-esteem and building resilience. Children gravitate to those with whom they have strong connections and bonds and, generally speaking, they will respond and interact more with adults who take a full interest in their lives (Grimmer, 2021).

Strategies you can implement in practice to support attachment

- Be an emotionally available, caring and loving educator.
- Use calm boxes to support children when they are dysregulated. Calm boxes include 3–5 of a child's favourite items that are known to help calm and distract.
- Use photos of children's families around your setting; this could be in a scrapbook, on small-world blocks or in frames. However you choose to provide this, you can look at photographs of the child's family, talk about their loved ones and reassure them they will be back soon.
- If a child finds it challenging to transition from their family member, allow them to bring a scarf that smells of that person into the setting. Smell often triggers memories, emotions and a feeling of safety.
- Prioritise feeling safe – children need to feel safe; when they feel safe, they are calm, regulated and ready for learning.

Adverse childhood experiences, such as abuse or neglect, can also affect a child's development, leading to behaviours that overlap with SEND. Trauma-informed practices are essential for educators in these cases, ensuring they provide the support children need while considering the impact of past experiences.

Unprecedented life events such as war or the COVID-19 global pandemic will disrupt a child's life in an unimaginable number of ways, worsening existing challenges but also creating new ones. Children experiencing these may face isolation, upheaval, loss of close family members and much more, all of which can disrupt their learning or even lead to regression in their development.

So how do we distinguish SEND from other needs? This is a good question as it is critical for ensuring that children receive the most effective support. Misinterpreting behaviours or challenges as SEND when they could be something else could risk a child either being over supported or not supported enough. We need to apply a holistic, informed approach and have a strong understanding of the root causes of children to support their growth and success.

- Use tools that evaluate the whole child, including their own environment, experiences and cultural background.

- Engage with families to understand the child's history and contextual factors that influence their behaviour.
- Work alongside other professionals in EAL, mental health and trauma-informed practices.
- Ensure that all educators are fully trained with the knowledge to differentiate between SEND and other factors, which could reduce the likelihood of a misdiagnosis.

Conclusion

Early identification of SEND is not just best practice – it is a foundational principle that underpins inclusive, effective, and compassionate early years education. By recognising and responding to developmental needs as early as possible, educators, families and professionals can work collaboratively to provide timely, targeted support, that significantly enhances a child's learning, development and overall well-being.

Children are more likely to thrive when their needs are understood and met early, families feel empowered and supported, and educators are better equipped to create inclusive environments that celebrate diversity and promote equity. Not only does early intervention support children in the moment but it can also reduce the need for more intensive support later.

Early identification of SEND is a powerful tool in ensuring that children receive the support they need to succeed. Educators must adopt a proactive, inclusive approach, work collaboratively with families, and use available resources such as the DfE Early Years SEND Assessment Toolkit, developed by Dingley's Promise, to guide their practice. By recognising the unique strengths and needs of each child early in their development, educators can create an environment where every child can thrive and lay the foundation for life-long learning, resilience, and success.

> **Reflection time**
>
> How do you engage families to understand their child's learning?
>
> What next steps would you take if you felt a child was not making anticipated progress with their learning?
>
> Can you think of a time you might have thought a child had SEND but it turned out to be something else? What would you do differently?

References and further reading

Bowlby, J. (1975). *Separation: Anxiety and Anger*. Harmondsworth: Pelican Books.

Department for Education. (2015) Special Educational Needs and Disability Code of Practice: 0 to 25 Years [Available at: https://www.gov.uk/government/publications/send-code-of-practice-0-to-25].

Department for Education & Dingley's Promise. (2024) *SEND Assessment Guidance and Resources* [Available at: https://help-for-early-years-providers.education.gov.uk/support-for-practitioners/send-assessment].

Department for Education, Grenier, J., & Pacy, M. (2023) *Integrated Reviews* [Available at: https://help-for-early-years-providers.education.gov.uk/support-for-practitioners/integrated-reviews].

Grimmer, T. (2021). Developing a Loving Pedagogy in the Early Years: *How Love Fits with Professional Practice* (1st ed.). Routledge.

Payne, S. (n.d.) 'A Beginners Guide to: Supporting English as an Additional Language EAL'. *Tapestry Beginners Guides* [Available at: https://tapestry.info/beginners-guides/].

4

Monitoring and assessment

Meggie Fisher

> **KEY DEFINITIONS**
>
> Assessment: A method through which we determine the perceived stages of development of a child at different points.
>
> Statutory: Required due to a formal written law.
>
> Celebratory approach: Focusing on skills achieved and the child's interests when exploring their development, rather than documenting perceived deficits in the child's development.
>
> SMART goals: Setting out goals or targets which are specific, measurable, achievable, relevant and time-bound. By considering these specifics, you create goals that are more likely to be achieved and the measurement of this achievement is clear.

Introduction

The monitoring and assessment of anything provides us with feedback and reflection opportunities to determine how something is working. When we think about the developing child, we know that all children develop at different rates and in different patterns. There are some key indicators in children's development which support us in identifying where children may require additional support or further consultation with a variety of professionals. As previously discussed in "Chapter 3: Early identification" the recognition of these critical points will have the most effective impact when identified and supported from an early point.

As educators, the joy in our role comes from supporting the development of children, engaging in their play, and teaching them new skills as we spend time together. It doesn't, however, stem from completing mountains of paperwork to ensure that the development we know we are achieving is identified, named, and tracked on a granular level. In 2021, it was recognised by Ofsted that a reduction in paperwork was required, and educators should focus on spending time with their children getting to know their strengths and interests and supporting their development in the moment. One challenge that educators continue to face, however, is how to enjoy this time spent with children with SEND when they still feel continued pressure to track and monitor progress in order to apply for formal assessments or funding.

The assessment process

Dynamic assessment of children is crucial to building a view of the child as a whole individual. Typically, this may include on-entry baseline assessment, mentally observing the ways in which they approach play, written observations, short or narrative recording of significant learning moments, formative and summative assessments. You must ensure you complete statutory assessments, such as the Progress check at age 2 and Early Years Foundation Stage Profile, within the required time frames and utilise other assessment methods to ensure you record what helps you support the child, any significant observations and key information you may require at a later date.

Types of assessment:

- **Baseline:** A developmental review completed with parent/carer views when a child begins attending early years provision.
- **Observations:** These may be mental or written and require the expertise of the professionals working with a child, to determine what they are seeing from the child with respect to their needs and development.
- **Summative Assessments:** These are often written at predetermined points of the year and provide a summary of the child's learning milestones against a chosen framework or guidance document.
- **Progress Check at Age 2:** Early years providers are legally obligated to complete this summary of development between the ages of 2 and 3 years as a key indicator of whether a child is on track with anticipated developmental milestones. It is best practice to integrate this with the health visitor Two Year Review.
- **Reception Baseline Assessment:** A short assessment completed within the first six weeks of a child starting reception; this is completed by reception teachers in school-based provision.
- **Early Years Foundation Stage Profile:** Is a summary of a child's learning as they come to the end of the foundation stage, the final school term after the child has turned 5 years old. The child's learning must be assessed against the Early Years Foundation Stage Early Learning Goals.

Approaching support for a child with emerging or identified SEND often starts with assessment, in line with the assess, plan, do, review cycle. It may be through observing that you have assessed a potential need in a child or when completing your standard cycle of written assessments, you recognise that a child is not meeting the same developmental milestones as their peers. These are crucial moments in which we must act to ensure early identification and support are given.

Methods of assessment: how?

There are many methods and tools to support you through assessment. Keeping the child at the centre of what we do is important and so often assessing through play-based techniques will build a comprehensive narrative that describes the child's strengths, interests and skills. To build this narrative you may choose to refer to the characteristics of effective teaching and learning (CoETL), schematic play, Leuven scales and gathering any other knowledge you have of the child. You may also assess the child against a set of criteria to determine what stage they are at with their development. We know that development is not a strictly linear process and that all children will develop at different rates, so it is important to take a positive strengths-based approach to your documented assessment. Tools such as "Development Matters" or "Birth to Five" are commonly used frameworks to support the understanding of child development; however, when identifying a child with emerging needs, you may need to consider more tailored frameworks such as the DfE Early Years SEND Assessment Toolkit, developed by Dingley's Promise.

Characteristics of effective teaching and learning

The characteristics of effective teaching and learning break down the way in which children learn into three key learning behaviours:

- Playing and Exploring (engagement).
- Active Learning (motivation).
- Creative and Critical thinking (thinking).

When observing children, it is a simple tool to use to follow how an individual child is learning and how they explore, make decisions and express interests. Early Years Educators can observe children within adult-led teaching moments as well as when they are actively engaged in their own child-led opportunities to identify CoETL. This will support understanding of the child as an individual and guide what support strategies the child may be most receptive to.

> ### Putting this into practice
>
> *Medhi has sensory processing challenges and avoids most messy play experiences. You regularly observe Medhi playing with the lions; he will often gather all the ones he can find in the room, look at books with lions in the pictures, and carry the lions around in his pockets. By understanding what engages Medhi (the lions), you can use these within messy play opportunities and demonstrate ways in which the lions may touch the new textures as you encourage Medhi to engage.*

40 *Early years inclusive practice for children with SEND*

Schematic play

Within early years we refer to schemas as a way to observe the way in which children learn. A schema is a pattern of reappearing behaviour which allows a child to explore as well as develop ideas and thoughts throughout their play and exploration. As an early years educator, you can observe, identify, and understand schemas that in turn develop a better understanding and awareness of each individual child and their needs and interests as well as their way of thinking.

Early years educators need to be able to understand and differentiate schematic play patterns to support the way in which the individual child explores and develops ideas. The nine types of Schematic Play are reflected in Figure 4.1. It is important to remember that schematic play presents itself as repeated patterns of behaviour which some educators can be quick to identify as a sign of SEND. Through your wider initial assessment of a child, you should be able to determine if repeated behaviours are solely stemming from a child's schema or if there are additional indicators that the child may have emerging SEND needs.

Each schema of play can be supported and encouraged in different ways. By understanding more about the basics of each schema, you can create baskets of resources readily available to meet that play pattern. For example, having a basket of balls which can be thrown in a safe space, or a basket of fabric for children to wrap around themselves or other favourite items like a comforter.

Leuven scales

Another useful tool is the Leuven scale. They can be used to break down a child's emotional well-being and involvement into five easy-to-follow stages. Children who are typically within levels 4 and 5 are more likely to be able to grasp information and learn successfully. It is

Figure 4.1 The nine types of schematic play

recognised that the Leuven scales can be used throughout a child's educational journey and are not just limited to their early years' education.

The well-being element looks at the extent to which children can feel at ease, be instinctive, and show self-confidence. It is an essential element of emotional intelligence and supports the development of good mental health. When looking for signs of well-being, you should consider how open and receptive they are to new inputs, how relaxed and free they seem, whether they radiate confidence, and how they are exuding joy and enjoyment.

1. **Extremely Low:** The child is clearly having a difficult time and doesn't feel happy in the setting. There are almost no instances of "true" pleasure. They are not at ease and are primarily anxious or tense. Their contact with the environment is difficult and they may present threatening behaviours towards others.
2. **Low:** The child shows elements of level one, but these are less pronounced.
3. **Moderate:** A child is neither happy nor unhappy. Moderate children are often indifferent and are rarely outspoken, positively or negatively. They're rarely excited, and social interactions with other children are pretty basic. There are few moments of real satisfaction.
4. **High:** A child shows elements of level 5, but these are less pronounced.
5. **Extremely High:** They feel like a "fish in water". They express emotions that are mostly positive, are clearly having fun, and laugh a lot. They enjoy being in their environment and interacting with peers, and their presence often positively affects the group dynamic. They show signs of strong emotional regulation: any anger, unhappiness, or fear quickly subsides.

The involvement element looks at the extent to which our children are learning or working to their full abilities. Particularly, it can indicate whether a child is interested, concentrating, and engaged in the activities they are taking part in. You should look out for facial expressions (do you stick your tongue out when you're really concentrating?!), how persistent they may be, how "in the zone" the child appears, and signs of satisfaction with what they are achieving.

1. **Extremely Low:** They often don't engage in activities at all, appear absent-minded and stare a lot. Activities that do occur are short-lived and purposeless. They usually lack dedication, get easily distracted, and don't pay much attention to their surroundings.
2. **Low:** A child shows elements of level one, but these are less pronounced.
3. **Moderate:** On first glance, the child can seem busy, but on closer inspection it's clear they're not really absorbed in what they're doing. They can pay attention, but they're rarely fully absorbed and struggle to concentrate. They often act routinely and their activities can be short-lived as they're easily distracted.
4. **High:** A child shows elements of level 5, but these are less pronounced.
5. **Extremely High:** These children are typically highly engaged in their activities. These children make decisions quickly and without hesitation. They demonstrate focus, dedication, interest and commitment without easily getting distracted.

It is important that we deeply consider how the child is engaging and investing in their tasks. Leuven scales should not be used as a tick-box exercise but as a guide to developing your understanding of how deeply the child engages and seeks joy within their play. For our children with SEND, recognising their Leuven levels can support you in developing your strategies which encourage their involvement and therefore their opportunities for deeper learning.

One-page profile

An effective method of gathering this information you are learning about a child is through a one-page profile. An example of a one-page profile is provided in Figure 4.2. This creates a clear outline of who the child is as an individual and will enable the key person, and others engaging with the child, to consider the child's strengths, interests and play patterns regularly to ensure the support provided is impactful for the child.

A one-page profile should include:

- The child's name and photo.
- What they enjoy or what makes them happy.
- How they might communicate or how you can communicate with them.
- Their play patterns or types of play, with consideration to CoETL and schematic play.
- What may upset them, or they might find challenging.
- Consistent support that would enable them to confidently access their learning.

Remember some of this information may change over time, so use regular opportunities with parents to discuss changes in interests, challenges and communication strategies to ensure you keep a child's one-page profile up to date.

A joined-up approach to assessment

Working with families

Working with families is a fundamental part of supporting children. For some, this may be the first conversation they have had regarding their child, and they may be reluctant to engage. It is key that when speaking to parents, we avoid using too much jargon, which can confuse or intimidate them, and to make sure we have everything we need to enable the family to gain confidence in what we are discussing. When building relationships, it is imperative that we allocate time to really get to know the family, whilst also allowing the family to get to know you as an individual. This builds the foundation of a trusting relationship as you move forward to support their child. When getting to know the family, it is an ideal opportunity to discuss and document their aspirations for their child, as well as discussing the child's own aspirations and what is important to the child right now.

At the very beginning, it is important that collectively you have set out the expectations for meetings. In order to monitor progress and to have detailed conversations, it is beneficial to meet termly, and by using the assessment framework, this enables early years

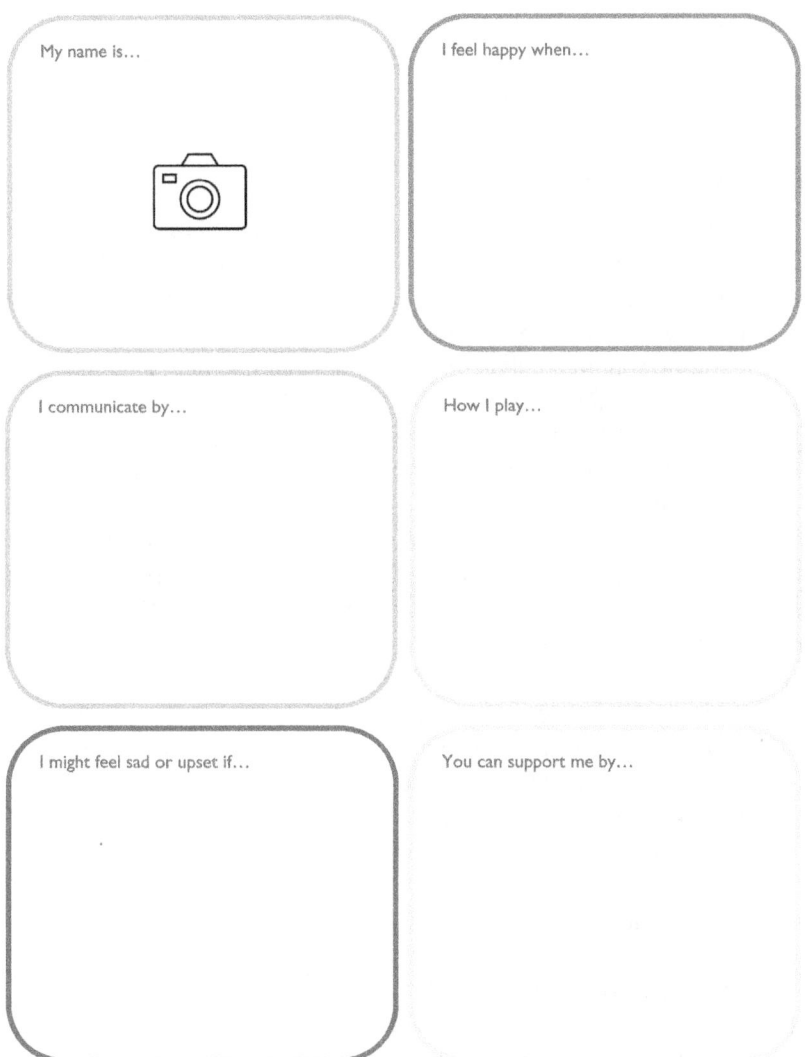

Figure 4.2 Dingley's Promise version of a one-page profile

educators to really see the progress made, explore the child's strengths, and consider relevant focus areas for the following term. Individual Support and Achievement Play Plans (SAPPs) enable you to document the current focus areas for the child, and it is important that the parent or carers' input is detailed within the SAPP document. This enables collaborative working whilst also giving the family the opportunity to fully understand how their child is developing as well as how they are being supported.

When meeting with parents and settings, we need to ensure that it is clear how information sharing with respect to other professionals and their reports is carried out. This will ensure professionals know the setting that the child attends and that they have the appropriate contact details to have clear communication. Enabling parents to understand this from the start also gives them time to prepare themselves for initial conversations with professionals as well as what to expect moving forward.

Working with professionals

To create a holistic approach to support for a child, it is important that all professionals working with the child and their family have a shared vision for that child's future. Different professionals provide support in different ways and will have specialist training to support the areas of need. When all professionals supporting a child and family collaborate and effectively share information, a full picture of support can be built and consistency in the strategies provided can be achieved.

If a child joins your setting with an already identified need, it is vital that you use your 'getting to know the family' paperwork to discuss the child's and family's needs, as well as the professionals already involved with the child. Where possible, gather the most recent reports from these professionals as soon as the family is able to, so that your setting-based support can enhance what has already been identified by others. Parents and carers should be encouraged to let any professionals they are already working with know about the early years provision their child is attending, so that meetings, information sharing, and visits can be coordinated when needed.

Where a child attends another early years provider, it is also key to ensure both settings share information effectively so that support strategies put into place are consistent for the child and messages shared with the family are also consistent. This may include integrating your development reviews so that both key people can share what they see from the child and are in alignment with their views.

Key practices for working with professionals:

- Timely information sharing.
- Integrated developmental reviews and assessments.
- Coproduction of support plans.
- Consistency of language used and messages shared with families.
- Sharing successes, challenges and ideas to further support the child.

 Case study: how working closely with professionals has embedded strong inclusive practice for all children

Within our Dingley's Promise centres, many of our children see a Speech and Language Therapist (SaLT). During these visits, the key person makes sure they are available to the therapist, so that they can discuss progress the child is making and share further information about the child's interests and skills. This enables the therapist to develop a deeper understanding of the child and to discuss how previous recommendations have been implemented, seeing what has and hasn't been impactful for the child, enabling them to better tailor future recommendations. Having these professional conversations has enabled us to see great progress in learning for many of our children with their commmunication development.

Through conversations with the SaLT, the team have been able to embed aided language boards across the whole setting, which has benefited all children not just those receiving speech therapy. The inclusion of these communication boards has seen children able to access communication across different areas of the centre and effectively share their thoughts and feelings with those around them.

Play-based learning and assessment

Play is the opportunity for children to become capable, do things themselves, grow their autonomy and learn how to learn. It is through play that children become capable and competent learners no matter their special educational needs or disabilities. For our children with SEND it is vital to remember that play is the primary method for learning and that our children should be provided with the same amount of opportunity to experience this. As we implement strategies to support a child, we must consider how these incorporate play and can be done with the child, not to or for them.

Language of assessment

Often assessing children with SEND has resulted in a deficit-based approach regarding the skills the child has not yet acquired and tasks they cannot complete. This has multiple negative effects on all involved in the process. For the child, there is a constant focus on what they cannot do, and the joy of the child's own interests can become lost in the focus to "improve" these areas of concern for the child. For the parent, they often hear constant messages about why their child is not like others their age and skills they haven't learnt, leading some to believe they may never learn, and this can have a negative impact on their own well-being and on their ability to promote their child's well-being and positive view of themselves. For professionals, they can lose sight of the child as a unique individual and begin solely regarding them as their area of need or disability as opposed to a child who can flourish with the right support. With this in mind, we recommend a strengths-based approach to language and a small adjustment in mindset which can have a big impact on the team working with the child.

> ### Putting this into practice
>
> *Instead of saying "Amari is non-verbal and doesn't listen to stories", a strengths-based assessment would say "Amari uses his communication boards and Makaton*

> independently and has a select few favourite books he likes to look at and share with his key person".
>
> This approach simply focuses on observing the child and noting what it is that they can and are doing without preconceived judgements of their skills and interests. This strengths-based language can be used during written observations as well as assessments, supporting the promotion of a child-centred approach.

Recording learning

Written observations may be beneficial in gathering a play-based assessment of a child's skills. This may take a narrative format in which a child's achievements are the focus, with consideration for strengths-based language. By utilising written observations in this way, you will find that the evidence required to meet any local authority funding applications or statutory assessments can be easily gathered from the documentation you have been ordinarily keeping to monitor and support a child, reducing pressure on your setting.

Observation example

11th April 2025: Child A, written by Key Person H.
H and I explored the sound book listening to all the different animal noises which made me smile and laugh. When the sound stopped, I said "again", and H pressed the button again which made me smile. I pushed myself up on my knees and stayed in the crawling position for a few minutes!
Characteristics of Effective Teaching and Learning: **Playing and Exploring**
Finding out and exploring   ✓ Showing curiosity about objects, events and people   ✓ Engaging in open-ended activity   ✓ Showing particular interests
Active Learning
Being involved and concentrating   ✓ Showing high levels of energy, fascination   Enjoying achieving what they set out to do   ✓ Showing satisfaction in meeting their own goals

This observation demonstrates that Child A can express happy emotions, use single words to communicate wants and understands simple ways to interact with familiar people. It also shows that Child A is making positive development physically by being able to balance in a crawling position for an extended period of time.

Highlighting the CoETL helps to demonstrate the ways in which the child is choosing to play so that future planning can spark their engagement in a similar way and then extend this further.

Assessment guidance and toolkit

Children will develop at their own unique rates, and not every child will follow a "typical" pattern of progression of development. This, however, does not limit a child's ability to make progress or take away from focusing on the child's individual strengths. The DfE Assessment guidance and toolkit produced in collaboration with Dingley's Promise was designed to aid in identifying needs as early as possible to support the implementation of high-quality early intervention. The simple framework of the toolkit aimed to reduce admin time and the duplication of paperwork within early years settings, freeing up time that could be spent supporting children with SEND and their families.

The assessment guidance contains:

- An assessment tool for each area of need and examples of how to use it.
- A one-page profile (as mentioned above).
- A Support and Achievement Play Plan template.
- SMART goals sheet to set short-term targets.

The assessment guidance introduced a new assessment tool centred around the four broad areas of need as reflected in Figure 4.3. These are further divided into three sub-sections, which allow you to see if there are particular areas of development that may need deeper focus.

It uses statements that reflect positive language and views, with the child working towards a series of "I can" statements. The focus of this language embeds educator thinking about what the child is able to achieve and how. It also considers the language used to assess these statements so that it is clear and simple to make a judgement.

Emerging: The child is showing some interest or awareness of this skill.
Supported: The child can achieve this skill with support from an adult.
Independent: The child can consistently achieve this skill on their own without additional support.

By using this language, we are able to focus on the progression of the skill and what the child can achieve over the time they are being supported.

Support and achievement play plans (SAPPs)

To support children with varying SEND needs, it is still important to include a termly Support and Achievement Play Plan (SAPP) which outlines the long-term goals as decided between

48 Early years inclusive practice for children with SEND

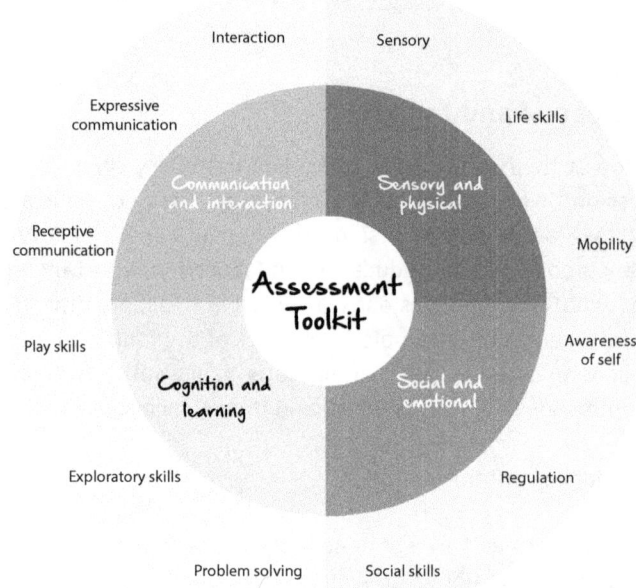

Figure 4.3 Areas of development covered within the SEND Assessment Guidance

the family, key person, SENCO and other relevant professionals, and how this is broken down into small step focuses for the coming term. Whilst we recommend these be reviewed and updated termly, it is important to remember that SAPPs may require reviewing sooner, should you feel a child is achieving the goals they were working on and no longer benefiting from the support outlined within the current version of the plan.

Within a SAPP, the following information should be included:

- Child's details (name, date of birth, funding entitlement, shared provision name if applicable).
- Provision details (name, key person, SENCO).
- Other professionals involved (name, job role, contact details).
- Date support started.
- Long-term goals for the child (consider voice of the child, parent, educator, other relevant professionals).
- Consistent strategies of support (these may not be goals you are working towards but strategies the child responds to or benefits from to support their ability to access learning).
- Up to four SMART goals that will support the child for the next term (12 weeks).

Monitoring and assessment

Support and achievement play plan

Child's name:	DoB:	Funding:	I have a one-page profile Y / N
Setting:	SENCo:		Key person:
Areas of need (please identify primary and secondary needs)			
Communication and interaction	Cognition and learning	Social and emotional	Sensory and/ physical
I attend another setting Y / N	Setting name:	SENCo:	Key Person:

The professionals supporting me are:			
Service	Professional	Job role	Contact details

Long term goals and aspirations (consider voice of the child, parent, practitioner, other relevant professionals)

Consistent support strategies that I will benefit from

My SMART goals

number: Plan

Date	Goal	How you can support me	Review
			Date:
Parent sign & date:	Key person sign & date:	SENCo sign & date:	
			Date:
Parent sign & date:	Key person sign & date:	SENCo sign & date:	
			Date:
Parent sign & date:	Key person sign & date:	SENCo sign & date:	
			Date:
Parent sign & date:	Key person sign & date:	SENCo sign & date:	

My SMART goals - EXAMPLE   Plan number 1

Date	Goal	How you can support me	Review
May 2025	To engage with a familiar person in a play situation such as rolling balls or cars back and forth once per session.	• Stand or sit in front of me so that I know you are trying to engage with me • Have fun with cars or balls where I can see you playing • Play alongside me, copying what I do • Use simple repeated language as you encourage me to play, "My turn, roll the ball, your turn, roll the ball"	Date:
Parent sign & date:		Key person sign & date:	SENCo sign & date:
May 2025	To follow instructions to recognise when I must have my nappy changed by a familiar adult.	• Key person or buddy to complete nappy changes • Use object of reference, nappy, to show me when it is time for a nappy change. • Sing the nappy song to support my moving from my play to the changing area • Use positive language and facial expressions around nappy changes, and to talk to me throughout to make me feel comfortable during these changes.	
			Date:
Parent sign & date:		Key person sign & date:	SENCo sign & date:

Putting this into practice

Supporting emerging SEND identified during a Progress check at age 2

The Early Years Foundation Stage (EYFS) progress check at age 2 remains a legal requirement for all children, and it is important that this is used as a review tool to assess any emerging needs that have yet to be identified. Working with parents to ensure they have attended their health visitor check at age two is also crucial to empowering them in supporting and advocating for their own child and their needs. You may also wish to liaise with the Health Visiting Team to complete this check together, integrating the views of the parent, health visitor, and key person/ SENCO which would enable clear communication between all and time to create a plan of support should this be needed for the child.

During an integrated two-year check, you feel a child is not working towards the anticipated communication milestones. The Health Visitor has also expressed that there may be a potential delay, and the parents had not realised that their child may be experiencing a delay; however, they are pleased it has been identified and are keen to know what support you can offer.

Using the Assessment tools, you can break down the skills the child is achieving and look towards what a child's priorities for support are and how you can aid with this.

Monitoring child progress

Every child's development journey is unique. Monitoring the progress children are making helps you to see where you may need to focus additional support or make adaptations to your environment and teaching.

Monitoring the development of all children within your care, can enable you to recognise trends and patterns in development which will further enhance your provision. For example, if you recognise patterns of strengths or challenges within a group of children, you can reflect on your team members and your environment, to ensure the training they receive and the set-up you have created is supporting children to progress.

Monitoring an individual child's progress over time enables you to recognise areas of need where they may require further support, but also spotlights their strengths by recognising areas in which they make continuous good progress. This information can be utilised to tailor support strategies at home and in the setting, make adjustments to the environment and highlight where additional information may need to be sought. Additional information may include training for team members to better understand a child's needs, further conversations or referrals to other professionals for specialist advice, or additional assessment information that may need to be gathered through observation or alternative assessment documentation.

You can utilise the assessment toolkit to clearly see the progress a child is making by monitoring the number of emerging, supported, or independent "I can" statements you have recorded. See the completed example of the Dingley's Promise Sensory and physical assessment tool in Figure 4.4.

Putting this into practice

An example of using the assessment tool

On recognising that Verity's physical development was not where you anticipated, you use the sensory and physical tool from the assessment toolkit to better understand her development. You hold discussions with her family to see if there are any differences in skill at home compared to nursery and you are confident that you have completed the assessment tool accurately.

Due to her age, you encourage Verity's family to engage with their Health Visitor for her progress check at age 2 and offer to join any conversations to support this health check. You are able to put support in place for Verity, and you continue to use the assessment tool to monitor her progress.

You see small steps of progress each time you assess Verity and are able to share these with the family. When they share that she is now sleeping for longer than two hour periods overnight, you all celebrate this win together!

As you have more closely observed Verity's play, you start to recognise a rotation schema. As you experiment offering different resources, you are able to discover what catches her attention and use these to plan further next steps.

Over time, this planning and support help Verity to make good progress with her physical skills alongside the support from other external professionals now involved with the family.

Sensory and physical

My name is: **Verity**
My DOB is: **21/07/2022**
My key person is: **Sabina**
My communication method is: **Makaton and some babbling**

Mobility			Life skills			Sensory		
I can crawl/ shuffle/ roll from one place to another	I can move in a variety of ways on two feet with or without a support aid	I can drink from an open top cup without support	I can navigate fastenings to aid me to dress myself, such as zips, buttons and clips	I will engage with new textures with interest	I can adjust my environment to meet my sensory needs, such as switching off lights, putting on ear defenders, removing uncomfortable clothing
E S I	E S I	**(E)** S I	E S I	E **(S)** I	E S I
I can move my arms/ legs across my body, crossing my midline	I can move around a room by cruising/ using an adult for support	I can feed myself with some success using hands or cutlery	I co-operate with dressing	I repeat actions which achieve a familiar outcome	I can express discomfort towards a sensory experience
E **(S)** **(I)**	E S I	E **(S)** I	**(E)** S I	E **(S)** I	E **(S)** I
I can grasp objects within my reach	I can put weight through my feet, this may be using an appropriate support aid	I try new foods during mealtimes	I can sleep for periods of two hours of longer	I respond positively to games involving physical touch or movement	I can respond in different ways to different sensory opportunities
E **(S)** I	E S I	E **(S)** **(I)**	E **(S)** I	E S **(I)**	E **(S)** I
I can move parts of my body in response to stimuli	I can sit using an appropriate support	I can open my mouth for feeding/ drinking	I can brush my gums/ teeth appropriately	I can close my fist around given objects	I am interested in exploring new experiences
E S **( )**	**(E)** **(S)** I	E S **(I)**	**(E)** S I	E S **(I)**	E **(S)** I

21/07/2022

E - Emerging S - Supported I - Independent

	Date completed	Completed by	Development growth	How I play (Play types, CoETL, Leuven levels)
Start point	23/10/24	Sabina	29/72	I will play with what I know with more confidence.
Review 1	30/01/25	Sabina	35/72	Playing with balls gets best engagement from me
Review 2	28/04/25	Sabina	47/72	Emerging rotation schema
Review 3			/72	
Review 4			/72	
Review 5			/72	

Figure 4.4 Completed example of the Dingley's Promise version of the sensory and physical assessment tool

Conclusion

Assessing and monitoring children is key to understanding their development and how to support them to succeed. However, assessments do not have to be rigid and formal and should, in fact be designed to capture a deep understanding of the child as an individual. It is important to focus on who the child is and getting to know their strengths and passions, as well as building an awareness of how you can provide additional support to enable them to thrive. Assessment does not need to look the same for each child, and you should use the various tools available to you that enable you to develop a better understanding of the child you are assessing.

Assessments should continue over time so that you can monitor the impact of the support you are putting into place; however, this can be achieved through noted observations as well as through structured summative assessments. You should also ensure you utilise the input of all those involved in supporting the child, to build a wider picture of what strengths and challenges they show in different situations and environments.

> **Reflection time**
>
> How do you approach assessing children's needs – how do you capture the child's strengths and interests and record your wider knowledge of the child?
>
> How many different types of paperwork do you complete for each child? Can you use fewer formats to reduce duplication for yourself and families?

References and further reading

Department for Education & Dingley's Promise (2024) 'SEND Assessment Guidance and Resources' [Available at: https://help-for-early-years-providers.education.gov.uk/support-for-practitioners/send-assessment].

Dubiel, J. (2016) *Effective Assessment in the Early Years Foundation Stage*. London, Sage.

Louis, S. et al. (2013) *Understanding Schemas in Young Children: An Introduction to Understanding and Supporting Schema Play in Young Children*. London, Featherstone.

Murphy, K. (n.d.) 'A Beginners Guide to: Self-directed Neurodivergent Play'. *Tapestry Beginners Guides* [Available at: https://tapestry.info/beginners-guides/].

5
Voice of the child

Abi Preston-Rees

> **KEY DEFINITIONS**
>
> Communication: The imparting or exchanging of information. This may be spoken, written, or use another medium such as exchanging objects or signing.
> Interaction: The engagement in a reciprocal action; you may notice "back and forth" or "serve and return" opportunities for communication or actions.
> Behaviour: The way in which someone responds to a particular stimulus.
> Body language: The conscious and unconscious movements and postures through which feelings and attitudes are communicated.

Introduction

When we consider the "voice of the child" we are automatically drawn to thinking about how they speak and use their voice to interact with others. However, voice should not just be about spoken word but include the thoughts, feelings, needs, wants, perspectives and views of the child, whether expressed through speech or other communicative methods. Within our everyday practice as early years educators, we need to reflect on how our decisions are informed and guided by the "voices" of the children we support. The United Nations Convention on the Rights of the Child (UNCRC) Article 12 states that "Every child has the right to express their views, feelings and wishes in all matters affecting them, and to have their views considered and taken seriously". This is true for all children, although listening to any child and truly hearing their "voice" can be both a simple and complex concept.

We must particularly consider the unique ways in which children with SEND communicate. They can be at a disadvantage in terms of having their voice heard and perspectives considered for multiple reasons. The Young Children's Voices Network identifies that children with SEND are subject to a much higher degree of adult intervention, meaning their scope for making day-to-day choices and decisions is severely limited. They have many things done to, and for them, and are significantly more vulnerable to abuse than non-disabled children. They are more likely to feel excluded from consultation processes because these are often based on written and spoken language, and family members and staff are more likely to see their roles as advocates rather than listeners. Having contact with multiple carers who lack the skills to understand their communication system can make their chances of expressing their views limited, thus affecting their self-esteem and mental well-being.

Recognising forms of communication

Often when listening to very young children who have limited communication or are pre-verbal, the meaning of their attempts at communicating is misunderstood. This is a challenge across early years in general as children develop their speech, language and communication skills, but is even more prevalent for children with SEND. To effectively listen to the "voice" of all children, understanding other methods of supporting communication is key. For educators to do this effectively, strong relationships with both the child and the family are essential. Families possess expert knowledge of their child; therefore, good communication between the setting and families from the start is paramount. By encouraging families to share knowledge about how their child provides clues as to what they want, whether this be through body language, signs or even specific noises, you will enable the promotion of children's self-esteem, giving them a "voice" which you are open to "listening" to. This is relevant for all children learning to acquire language and communication skills, but it is more significant for children who display cognitive understanding with limited communication; this partnership and shared understanding will help to reduce frustration the child may display due to not having their wants or needs met. Remember, behaviour is communication, and partnership working could be the key to decoding what is being communicated.

These elements of consideration for children with SEND make it even more important to encourage early years educators to reflect on the inclusivity of their provision in terms of capturing and responding to the child's voice, to ensure that children grow to be confident members of society who feel respected and have a strong sense of emotional well-being. Adults can often fear that they require specific expertise to listen to children with SEND. However, spoken language is only one of a range of methods that we use to communicate our thoughts, feelings, and ideas. Body language, facial expressions, and physical reactions such as laughing and crying, are just some of the ways in which we naturally express ourselves and communicate how we are feeling. Some new skills and resources may be needed alongside an attitude of respect and curiosity, to ensure that we are using all possible methods to allow children every chance of being understood.

Behaviour is a form of communication and is reliant on educators noticing and interpreting this behaviour correctly. Understanding children's behaviour and what they are trying to communicate, relies on those around them building and maintaining positive relationships to accurately interpret all communication attempts. This ideology is underpinned within the Key Person approach in The Early Years Foundation Stage and emphasises the importance of working with the family to get to know the child well, which in turn will lead to them feeling safe and secure in your care and able to use their "voice" to fully communicate their wants and needs in whichever method they prefer.

Remember to take note of some key features of communication:

- **Gestures or Actions:** These may be self-taught, copied from others or linked to familiar rhymes or songs.
- **Body Language:** Do they turn towards or away from certain things?
- **Emotions or Facial Expressions:** Can you determine when they are happy, excited, sad or unsure?
- **Sounds:** Do they use the same sounds regularly? Could certain noises be related to certain objects, wants or needs?

These features are normally present within every adult conversation or interaction; however, the prevalence of these features can be influenced by developmental level or specific needs amongst children. From a very young age, children will make vocalisations such as crying to communicate their need for food, sleep, or if they are in pain. Vocalisations refer to the expression of something in words or sounds, and as children develop, these noises become more and more deliberate as they attribute specific meaning to sounds. Making these vocalisations, however, is only one aspect of verbal communication; intonation or tone of voice plays a big role in understanding what is being communicated.

Communication challenges for children with SEND

Autistic children commonly find it more difficult to communicate non-verbally through gestures and facial expressions. This means that features of non-verbal communication displayed by these individuals may be more exaggerated than one typically expects, or they may adopt a neutral expression. It is important to consider the wider context of the child as their body language alone may not be a reliable indicator. Autistic children also commonly have difficulties in identifying the emotions of others, but they are still able to experience their own full range of emotions. This may be harder for educators to accurately identify, so it is important to get to know the child and build a trusting relationship so that subtle communication cues are not missed. Tone of spoken word can also be difficult to understand, as it is used to modify the meaning of words. Autistic people may understand and use words literally, and this can lead to misunderstandings in the intended meaning, both when listening and verbally communicating. This can cause frustration, and we must work hard not to discourage individuals from communicating but rather to build their confidence in expressing themselves using our knowledge and skills to help support and guide communication attempts.

Echolalia is common among young children. It refers to specific verbal speech which is "echoed" or repeated not necessarily in the appropriate context. This repetition and interest in a specific word or phrase can seem to be a very limited and non-functional use of language; however, it provides the opportunity to build more functional language skills through acknowledging their interests and introducing new concepts and words. By listening to them and accepting their interests, you will help to build their self-esteem and make them feel safe and understood, which can lead to more positive relationships and further communication and learning opportunities.

Immediate echolalia may look like:

Repeating Questions: "Do you want a drink?"; the child may respond by repeating, "do you want a drink?"
Repeating Answers: "Would you like the ball?"; the child may respond with "ball, ball".
Repeating Prompts: "Say, hello George"; the child may repeat "say hello George".

Delayed echolalia may look like:

Repeating Language from Television: "Chase is on the case" when they are asked to complete a task.
Repeating Lines from Songs: "I like to eat, eat, eat apples and bananas" when they are hungry and would like a snack.
Repeating Words from Specific Contexts: "It's time to go to the park" every time they want to go outside. Tune into what you do hear from the children you are supporting, looking for regular patterns in words or phrases they use and seek to understand what they may be communicating to you.

You should also consider the sensory input a child is receiving during social interactions. Communication is a rich tapestry of multisensory indicators, and communicative attempts adopt multiple types of communication within one single interaction. The combination of the types of communication used in each interaction, for example, verbal in conjunction with gestures and facial expressions, can be different each time. This presents a multitude of sensory information within every interaction, with no two interactions being the same. For a child who has sensory processing differences, this can make communicative attempts, especially typical back-and-forth conversation, overwhelming. Seek to use consistency and methods of communication the child is comfortable with as you build their confidence in navigating social interactions. Recognise where additional communication distraction can be reduced, such as background noise, which could be exacerbating sensory overload.

Building a communication rich environment

Exposing children to a range of communication methods allows them to learn new interaction skills in a positive environment. They will then be able to express themselves not just through spoken language but a variety of communication methods, ensuring that their "voice" is heard. The diagrams reflect the different communication methods which can be used to support a communication rich environment (Figures 5.1-5.6).

This approach presents greater opportunities to engage all children, but specifically those with SEND. Providing an environment rich in opportunities to communicate and which considers all senses, will put emphasis on capturing the voice of each child and giving them the best opportunity to choose a method that suits them, whilst being adaptable to meet their varying needs. The use of a communication board to provide this freedom of choice is shown in Figure 5.7. The diagrams below reflect the Makaton sign for sleep (Figure 5.8) and the accompanying symbol which can be displayed in the setting (Figure 5.9).

Figure 5.1 Consistency: offering the same forms of communication in as many situations as possible

Figure 5.2 Signing: (often Makaton but some children may learn sign-along or British Sign Language) signs and gestures should be used even if no children within your room rely on this to communicate. This will mean that everyone, adults and children, will be comfortable and confident in using signs to communicate should a child prefer this method

Figure 5.3 Visuals: real-life objects, photographs and symbols can all be used; different children will relate more to different visual representations. These can be used to create a timeline, choice boards or reinforce or provide context for spoken words. Make sure visuals are within the eyeline of the children!

Figure 5.4 Sensory input: can you reduce distractions such as background noise? Can you introduce rhymes or music to signify a transition such as when the garden or snack is available? Could you use scent to designate different areas of the room?

Figure 5.5 Situational understanding: use real-life objects and situations to develop understanding; situational comes before conceptual. Holding a cup whilst standing by the snack table at the same time every day will help a child to understand the words "drink time"

Figure 5.6 Use timers: these can be used to show a child how long is left before a transition must happen, such as going to change their nappy or sit down for a meal. They can also be used between children to negotiate turn taking and cooperation by showing each other the timer and understanding the expectation to wait

Figure 5.7 A visual timetable which includes symbols, photographs and objects of reference positioned at the height of the children. This enables them to access each visual to communicate their wants and needs to those around them, not just be communicated to

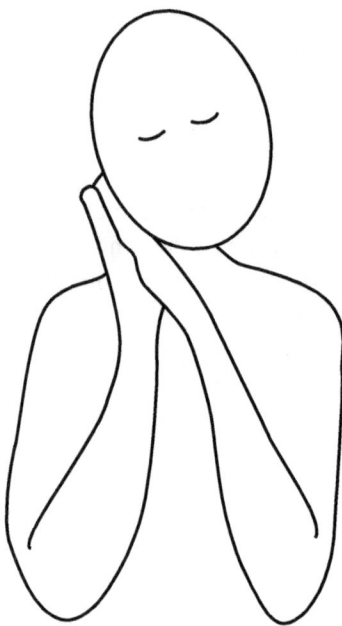

Figure 5.8 Makaton sign for sleep

Figure 5.9 Alongside the symbol for sleep

Communication through play

The concept of "play" provides an endless scope for both children to communicate and adults to listen. However, this is reliant on accurate interpretation of what the child is communicating. Quality interactions depend on a variety of play contexts led and initiated by the child. Role play, dance, music, singing, story time are some ways through which children commonly express themselves. It is the educators' role to observe and notice what the child is doing and what these actions could be communicating. By observing we can look and listen to children to ascertain: their current developmental level; their likes, interests, preferences and feelings; what they are learning through their play; how their personal experiences are reflected within their play. Listening to children and empowering them to communicate through play creates a continuous cycle of educators observing, reflecting on what can be learnt from this, and planning how the child's voice can be further embedded within provision. By reviewing and reflecting on observations, whilst considering the wider context of the child and environment, educators may find a multitude of potentially communicated messages through one single observation. Recognising these empowers children's ability to communicate choices, preferences, and interests, and by tracking the physical locations and resources that are accessed most, and removing, replacing or changing the set-up of items that are not commonly accessed, we can ensure that the environment is set up to encourage engagement and expression of self.

Voice of the child 61

So how do educators continue to identify and provide play opportunities with the most communicative potential? Children with SEND are more likely to have specific interests and sensory needs. Simple multisensory activities are most likely to be engaged with by a larger quantity and variety of children, regardless of developmental ability. Settings can do this by creating provocations allowing for children to experience and explore collections of items that interest and engage, providing an open-ended opportunity to explore, wonder and be creative, as demonstrated in the Seed to Sunflower provocation shown in Figure 5.10. An example of a provocation is something as simple as a treasure basket or curiosity boxes. These can combine multiple items that might link through shape, colour, season or experience. Children can explore and feel the objects in any way they choose, combining them, labelling or manipulating them in new and interesting ways. The adult can engage and use clear support strategies to enhance the opportunities for learning communication such as narrating the play, modelling simple language, using exciting sounds to engage the child and build their curiosity and wonder.

Here are a variety of provocations, designed to engage children across multiple senses and provide opportunities to expand their vocabulary and understanding of communication and interaction.

Play is a powerful tool for aiding development for many reasons. Encouraging play alongside these basic considerations will give children the best start at building on their use of language or communication attempts in meaningful contexts:

Figure 5.10 Seed to sunflower, Whatever next, When I build with blocks and Introducing loose parts provocations

A language rich environment providing a range of communication strategies and opportunities for interaction.	Communication friendly spaces purposefully set up spaces to increase children's opportunities and confidence to communicate.	Opportunities for songs and rhymes incorporating these not only within set routine times but also during free play in a variety of languages.	Multisensory experiences using the voice and body to explore actions and language.
Time to explore and recall through repetition of stories and activities and reviewing photos and videos.	An attentive communicative partner actively listening, asking open-ended questions, engaging often, being child led.	Opportunities to model listening and attention offering eye contact (but this is not essential for communication!), positive body language, getting down to their level.	Acquiring children's attention first before speaking using their name, allowing time for them to respond.
Building positive relationships with the child and family understand influences, strengths, and motivators to the child.	Providing things that are familiar and comforting to the child considering interests and high motivators which will offer opportunities to feel safe and able to engage.	Time and gaps for children to attempt to communicate opportunities for back-and-forth interaction with pauses and moments of silence.	Providing structured adult-led time working towards agreed targets and next steps to build confidence in using their "voice".

Individual communication methods

As children develop their understanding of communication and interacting with those around them, they may show a preference for a particular communication method or demonstrate skills that support the use of certain communication tools. As we recognise these, it is important to consistently offer these communication tools to the child, as shown in Figure 5.11, so that they are able to share their voice – imagine losing your voice and having no alternative method to be heard! It is vital that there are no excuses for communication tools to be missing or unavailable for periods of time, as these are a child's right and should be readily available. We should work closely with the family to support them in implementing strategies at home, and we should work with and follow the advice of any specialists involved, such as Speech and Language Therapists.

Communication boards and Alternative and Augmentative Communication devices (AAC) can be individualised to aid an individual child or can be more general and used by all children to make choices and express preferences.

Communication boards can be as simple as a laminated piece of paper containing symbols, photos and images familiar to children, or more complex through the use of electronic boards created and delivered via software on a tablet. Figure 5.12 shows a Communication Board being used in setting.

On the boards are symbols of common words, nouns, verbs and adjectives enabling the user to point at the symbols to either communicate single words or construct a sentence.

Voice of the child 63

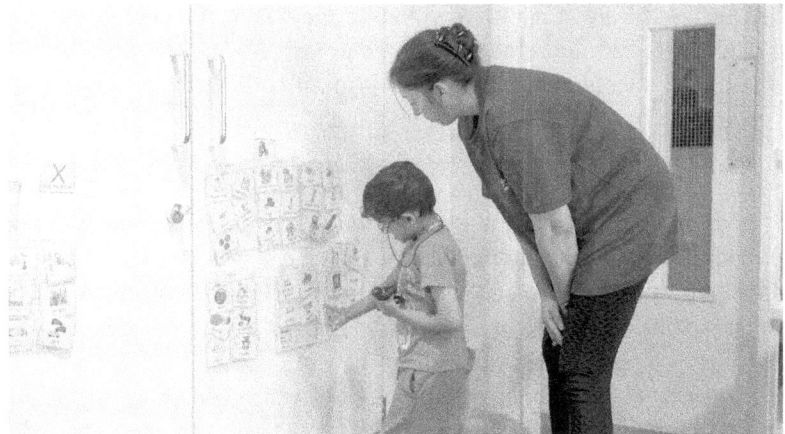

Figure 5.11 Using a choosing board

Figure 5.12 Using a communication board

Visuals can be available in languages other than English and can give a child a "voice", allowing them to visually express themselves in the moment to whatever degree they are capable of, whether this be making choices or having a general conversation.

Objects of reference are items that have meanings assigned to them and can be used if a child is not yet ready to use pictures of objects or activities or has a visual or other sensory difference. They aid understanding of verbal instructions by giving clues about what is going to happen next. For example, giving a child a nappy to show them they are going to have a nappy change, or a plate to show them that it is time for lunch. These objects need to remain consistent and be available for the child to also use to communicate to an adult that they would like something, for example, a cup to indicate they are thirsty or some leaves to show they want to go outside. Once a child is consistently able to recognise and use these objects to both understand what is happening and to make requests, pictures may be introduced to further develop their understanding, increasing the number when suitable, to allow more requests to be understood and communicated.

Recordable communication buttons can be used with pre-verbal children. They are most commonly used with those who have profound and multiple learning difficulties (PMLD) to increase their ability to communicate. They work by recording a simple word such as "more" so that the child can press it themselves or be supported hand-over-hand to communicate they want "more" of a food, toy or activity. Singular buttons as well as multi-buttons are available, providing opportunities for children to make choices. Visuals can also be inserted to offer meaning to what the child can communicate. Buttons are versatile and can be used to record single words, whole nursery rhymes, messages about the day enabling a child to join in and have their voice heard.

There are many more techniques or interventions which can be used in everyday practice to support communication development. Many of these may be used already within your setting:

Match +1 is a verbal communication strategy used to increase children's ability to create longer verbal utterances with more information. This works when an adult is listening and engaging with a child; the child may request "more", then an adult can respond with one extra word or piece of information, i.e. "more bubbles". This not only increases children's awareness and exposure to a range of vocabulary, but also models the use of language and the foundations of sentence structure. Whilst designed to be used verbally, this can be used with multiple methods of communication such as communication boards or Makaton.

Recasting in the context of verbal communication is a strategy used to refine pronunciation, grammar, and verbal language attempts, i.e. a child may ask an adult "where at", then an adult can repeat and recast this information accurately, reinforcing the correct pronunciation "where is the cat". This will not only improve spoken language skills but build self-esteem as the child knows they are being listened to.

Modelling refers to educators showing children how things work or can be done. In the context of communication development, modelling could involve an educator selecting a visual aid and handing it to another person to model how to complete a communication exchange, or playing with a resource such as blocks and signing "more" to ask for more blocks to build the tower higher.

Knock, knock what's in the box? is a communication game in which a few items are placed inside a box. The adult models and encourages the child to join in knocking and saying knock, knock what's in the box? before opening and retrieving one of the items. The adult then labels the item, providing simple language and other appropriate communication techniques such as Makaton. This game provides opportunities for educators to reinforce and gauge children's understanding and ability to communicate whilst equipping them with new words and vocabulary relevant to motivating items. The knocking on the box, retrieving and labelling the item is repeated until all the items in the box have been explored. This is not only useful in enhancing and developing children's communication but also their listening and attention skills whilst building their confidence.

Intensive interaction is a strategy used in a play-based way to reinforce listening, response, and communication among children with limited or no communication and those with learning difficulties or delays. It works by mirroring and producing the movements, body language, facial expressions and noises the child displays. It can help children to feel connected, as you engage and share in their thoughts and ideas in a way they can understand. It can help children to feel more aware of themselves, their bodies, the people around them and their environment, building self-esteem and self-worth. When comfortable, they may engage in two-way communication and begin to look and start copying the adult.

 Case study: giving a voice to Child Z

Intent

Our intention was to support Z, a quiet and observant child who joined Dingley's Promise in September 2022 at the age of 2. Z has a significant speech and language delay and primarily communicated through gestures and facial expressions. Her limited ability to express choices, feelings, and preferences often led to frustration and distress. We aimed to provide her with the tools and support she needed to express herself and feel understood.

Implementation

Initially, the team found it challenging to interpret Z's needs and emotions. It became clear that in order to support her effectively, we needed to respect her communication style and developmental stage.

Z's key person began by conducting regular observations, carefully noting her non-verbal cues – such as smiling, making eye contact, reaching for items, and guiding adults by the hand – to interpret her intentions and preferences. In response, we introduced a range of communication aids including visual supports, language-aided boards and Makaton. Along with observing and recognising her sensory processing differences in relation to the clothing on her body.

The key person used child-led play to build a trusting relationship and encourage communication. Activities such as repeated play with toy animals and water play revealed Z's sensory interests. By sitting with her at eye level, narrating her play, and consistently responding to her cues, staff created an environment where Z felt safe and empowered to express herself.

Impact

Introducing visuals provided Z with a reliable and meaningful way to communicate her needs and preferences. For the first time, she had a consistent method to express when she wanted something – or when she wanted more of a particular interaction. A personalised visual symbol book was developed for Z, which she was also able to use at home, ensuring continuity between settings. From feeling safe, secure and heard by the key person, she was able to manage her sensory differences with support, meaning she was regulated and more content.

As a result, staff were able to incorporate her preferences into daily activities and confidently assert that her voice was being heard – even if not spoken. Z's sense of control grew, and with it, her ability to engage more fully in her early years experience.

Conclusion

Listening to children and allowing them to use their "voice" is a fundamental right of the child. Listening acknowledges children's rights to be heard and for their views and experiences to be taken seriously. Additionally, listening influences our understanding of children's priorities, interests, and concerns. It can make a difference to how children feel about themselves and is a vital part of establishing respectful relationships with the children we work with. Every professional working with children should ensure that the child's voice is being heard and considered on matters that affect them.

Having meaningful engagement and interaction with a child leads to more successful outcomes, meaning that children become active social agents in their decision-making. If we do not listen actively to each child's voice, we convey to the child and others that we do not value the child's perspective, and ultimately, that we do not value the child. By choosing to act in this way, we teach children to be undemocratic: they learn that the individual's view is not important for the group. Yet, a person's view is integral to their identity, and developing a positive identity is fundamental to realising every child's rights. Listening to children's voices is essential and is even more important when engaging with children with SEND, in enabling their right to express their views on matters that affect them and to have their views considered in a meaningful way.

> **Reflection time**
>
> As you continue your journey to supporting the "Voice of the Child", consider how opportunities for reflection are built into daily practice and implemented in a planned and organised way to ensure that reflection is captured and acted on.
>
> How does your setting use children's "voices", views, and opinions not only in relation to children's participation in activities, but also in the values and structures of the organisation?
>
> Observe children in your setting; how do they communicate with adults and each other? Are there any barriers to communication that your children are experiencing?
>
> Could you implement different communication strategies to enable more children to have their voice heard?

References and further reading

Mary Dickins (2008). *Listening as a Way of Life: Listening to Young Disabled Children.* Young Children's Voices Network (https://www.ncb.org.uk/sites/default/files/uploads/files/NO17%2520-%2520listening_to_young_disabled_children.pdf).

Unicef – The Rights of Every Child – Article 12 131.-CRC-poster-A2-1pp-AW.pdf (https://www.unicef.org.uk/wp-content/uploads/2017/09/131.-CRC-poster-A2-1pp-AW.pdf).

www.makaton.org.

www.intensiveinteraction.org.

www.attentionautism.com.uk.

6

The inclusive team

Lee Friend

> **KEY DEFINITIONS**
> Team: A group of people who may have individual roles or tasks that contribute to achieving a common goal.
> Strengths: Skills in which a person or group of people are highly proficient and capable.

Introduction

Being part of an inclusive team means a collaborative and whole setting approach to inclusion which in turn improves the quality of the inclusive environment you provide for children and families.

When we support children, we rarely work as an individual; we almost always work as part of a team. Working as part of a team can take many formats depending on the set-up of your early years provision and the needs of each child. For leaders and managers, you are responsible for the staff team that works within your setting, creating a team of educators with mixed skills, education and experience. You may also have a network of other settings, childminders or early years providers, which together form a team who are working towards better outcomes for children in your area. As an educator, you are not only part of your staff team, but you may also be part of a specific team who work with and support a particular child and their family. The team supporting a child will look different based on their needs, family circumstances and the resources available within your local area.

It is important to understand who is involved with a child and their family and what their role in providing support is so that we can work together to provide a consistent and collaborative approach.

Who might be a part of a child's team?

At home	Setting based team members	Health professionals	Other external professionals
The child	Key person and buddy	Health visitor	Another setting, childminder or nanny
Parents/carers	SENCO	GP	Local authority support team
Siblings	Setting Manager or deputy	A range of therapists such as speech and language, occupational health or physical	Early Help team
Grandparents	Chef/cook	Specific medical professionals such as doctors or nurses	Social worker
Other close family members or friends	Outreach or family worker		Family support worker or Portage worker

One of the key parts of an early years educators role is the partnership they have with parents. Knowing their child's key person and having a trusting relationship where they feel confident and comfortable to share the highs and lows of parenting is so important. Parents and carers are so thankful for the experiences, opportunities, and development we provide for their children. Naturally, they are the advocates for their children and simply want the best for them. Often, parents may come to you for advice and support and it is vital that we are ready to provide this, or able to signpost parents towards support materials or other professionals who can guide them.

To read more about working with families, head to "Chapter 7: Family partnerships".

Being part of an inclusive team

When it comes to inclusion, it is absolutely critical that you promote and inspire inclusive practice across the entire setting regardless of your role, working with your team to recognise its importance and enable them to share in that vision. When the whole team is working towards the same vision, you can then ensure that the practical aspects of this vision become reality; following correct procedures, implementing training, delivering the organisations plans and strategy. The more it is done together, the more you can use skills and experiences of others to support the entire team.

Inclusion is everybody's business. The role you play within your team is key to ensuring consistent delivery of strong inclusive practice. It is important that every member of the team understands how to be inclusive and how to support each other in developing inclusive practices.

When planning and developing your environments and play experiences, it is important that you approach these with your inclusive ethos.

When working as part of a team, it is critical that everybody:

- Thinks about how to ensure their set-up is flexible and adaptable to the needs of all children.
- Actively encourages opportunities for children of all backgrounds and skill levels to engage.
- Recognises the impact of the resources available and the importance of representation.

These aspects are all key to developing strong inclusive provision but can only be impactful if each member of the team plays their part. You should remember that not everyone will have the same experience of practice, or confidence in implementing inclusion. You may not know the answer to everything, but that's why you have a team; work together to find the answer or a solution and utilise the strengths and skillsets of the whole team. This can help to build confidence, expose you to different experiences, and give the opportunity for others to coach and mentor. We all start from somewhere, and strong inclusive teams will only want to see you succeed in every opportunity that comes your way.

It is also vital that the children we work with see you as a positive role model for inclusive practice, as having positive role models will help the children to accept and expect inclusion in future life. Being part of a diverse workforce can create opportunities for children to recognise that everyone is different, and everyone deserves the opportunity to be a part of the community. This could include male educators who can be hugely positive role models – especially for those families who don't have a father figure in the household.Equally, female staff have the same effect for those families who may not have a female influence. We all want to be role models for our children to teach them the way things should be and to promote how to be proud and celebrate what makes them unique, what makes them tick as an individual and as a collective!

The role of the SENCO

The Special Educational Needs Coordinator (SENCO) should be a knowledgeable and experienced supporter of children with SEND and should be confident in the coordination of professionals involved with a child. They should have a secure understanding of the SEN Code of Practice, how this is implemented within their settings and how it supports settings to implement inclusive practice. A SENCO provides guidance and support to the team members working with children, to ensure effective support strategies are being implemented based on the child's individual needs.

Different types of early years provision have different requirements for the person undertaking the SENCO role. For example, maintained nursery schools require the SENCO to have Qualified Teacher Status (QTS) and to undertake the Masters-level National Award for Special Educational Needs Coordinator within three years of taking up the post. Whereas private, voluntary and independent settings only need to identify a level 3 qualified staff member as the SENCO with no additional qualification requirements. If you are a childminder, you may be part of an agency or work with a close network of childminders in your area, so you are able to share the SENCO role between you provided you have someone clearly nominated.

Key aspects of the early years SENCO role are:

1. Ensuring all practitioners in the setting understand their responsibilities to children with SEND and the setting's approach to identifying and meeting SEND needs.
2. Advising and supporting colleagues.
3. Ensuring parents are closely involved throughout and that their insights inform action taken by the setting.
4. Liaising with professionals or agencies beyond the setting.
5. Continually develop own practice.

The key person and buddy

As the key person or buddy of a child with SEND, you have a hugely important role to play in supporting them and their family. You will be instrumental in assessing the child's strengths and areas of support needed, and you will actively implement support strategies and adjustments to the environment to aid the child in accessing their learning. You will often be able to provide clear feedback on what works well for the child, as well as when strategies are ineffective or not quite tailored to the child's individual interests or needs. As you observe, engage with, and assess the child's development, you will be able to ensure that the support you are providing and the advice and interventions recommended by specialists and other professionals are having the desired positive impact.

The team around the child: working collaboratively

Children with SEND may have a range of other professionals external to your setting supporting them. For some children, this could be a large team, while for others it may only be one or two, but either way, a collaborative approach to working together is vital. Each professional will have unique insight into the child, based on their expertise and interactions with the child, and through this will be able to provide differing support as needed. As a group of professionals working together, communication and information sharing is vital; however, this can be challenging when working in a disjointed environment. Access to information and data sharing regulations ensures that children and families' privacy is maintained, but can be a barrier to joint working in some cases. You should work with parents and carers to support their understanding of how you will work with the other professionals involved and make them aware of the role they may play in sharing key contacts and supportive reports. This is also a prime opportunity to provide further family support, as professional reports can be intimidating or disconcerting for some families. We can provide a safe space to discuss their concerns or queries and demonstrate how the support recommended can be implemented in the setting and at home.

Where possible, inviting other specialists working with the child into the setting can provide valuable knowledge and insight into how you can provide a consistent approach. This can also enable you to learn from other professionals' expertise as they are able to demonstrate how recommended strategies can look or provide hints, tips and links to useful resources.

Leaders of inclusion

As a leader or manager within early years provision, it is critical that they lead by example when it comes to inclusive practice and promote and encourage inclusion through policies and procedures. The role of the leader of an inclusive team may take different directions based on the children and team members within the setting. For some educators, they need a leader who is the font of knowledge and training that they turn to for guidance when supporting children; others may need a shoulder to lean on when they are finding things challenging, and some need someone to remind them they are part of a team and they are doing an incredible job. For some parents, the leader or manager is the safe and familiar person that they feel most comfortable talking to; some will hold leaders accountable for the support their child is receiving in the setting, and for others the manager is the welcoming face that opens the door each session. Some leaders and managers also have multiple roles and so may be performing key person or SENCO duties alongside their management duties. Where they work across multiple teams and potentially multiple roles, they play a crucial role in developing and embedding inclusive practice within the setting. Each person in the team brings their own unique skills and interests which when collectively put together, create a diverse and well-established team. Pulling on the strengths of everyone can really help with sharing the workload and creating a culture where everyone has a voice to be able to actively play a part in the delivery and planning.

The benefits of recognising strengths:

- Empowers each individual to take ownership of their actions.
- Creates a team that is open to sharing ideas and collaborating to solve challenges.
- Boosts individuals' confidence and self-esteem.

Setting and understanding expectations is crucial for a team to work together; this can be achieved through:

- **Communication:** Clearly communicated expectations support everyone in understanding their roles and responsibilities; it is also beneficial to ensure everyone understands how this supports children.
- **Collaboration among Leaders:** A setting may have many different leaders working to promote inclusion; the manager, SENCO and room leaders are likely to be part of this. Working closely to understand "Ordinarily Available Provision" ensures that all teams are aligned as they support children with SEND.
- **Training and Meetings:** Use one-on-one discussions, team meetings, and training sessions to ensure that all team members have the opportunity to understand the vision and goals. Regular opportunities for discussion and revisiting training aids in embedding expectations and supporting everyone to develop their skills and knowledge.

Developing a reflective culture

Developing a reflective culture as a team is important to ensure that you are continuously implementing strong inclusive practice that supports the children in your setting at that moment. We have to reflect honestly and openly to consider whether we are as inclusive as we can be by looking at practice, ratios and funding access with an aim of being as inclusive as we can. Reflection can be done as an individual or group exercise. It can be presented as a formal document, but some great insights can also come from discussion during a lunch break or within a CPD session, as reflected in Figure 6.1. What is important is that reflections generate actions, whether this is celebrating great practice or taking steps to make improvements. Key benefits of reflection include:

- **Continuous Improvement:** Reflection allows the team to assess their practices and identify areas for improvement. This ongoing process helps in adjusting strategies and approaches to deliver best practice that is right for your children.
- **Team Support:** Encourage a supportive network where everyone can share ideas and experiences. Reflecting as a team enables different perspectives and experiences to be considered, aiding the creation of more inclusive and equitable environments.
- **Financial Efficiency:** Practice which focuses on the inclusion of all children reduces the need for one-to-one support as children's needs will be more readily met.

Continuous development of inclusive practices not only improves team understanding and confidence but also opportunities for children and potentially financial savings. By fostering an inclusive and reflective culture, a strong, motivated team can be created, well-equipped to support each other and the children in their care.

Figure 6.1 Team engaging in an outdoor learning CPD session

Another part of building an inclusive team is looking at the wellbeing of each member of that team. We've seen that the early years workforce has seen a rise in Educators, Managers and SENCOs leaving the profession and one of the common reasons for this is the lack of support. Educators recognise how critical the early years are for all children – but particularly for children with Special Educational Needs & Disabilities. It can really affect the trajectory of the rest of their lives. Supporting the child and their family can put a lot of pressure on our educators, and the responsibility of managing the transition to school – especially when the family are making decisions between mainstream and specialist provision – is a particular pressure point. Educators are juggling new settings, parents, professionals and fundamentally the child, responsible for ensuring that a decision which is in everyone's interests is made. Leaders and managers cannot fix everyone's problems, but they can be available and encourage communication and conversations which explore wellbeing, support and personal development.

For more on well-being see "Chapter 12: Wellbeing in early years".

Building your inclusive team: recruitment and retention

We have a duty to be inclusive of children with SEND in the early years. Not only is it morally right to welcome all children into your setting, but it is good for all children, adults and society too. There is also a raft of legislation directing and shaping how you and local authorities jointly provide early education for all children, and childcare that supports parents to work and train. When we think about what we do for children, it's important to ask ourselves whether we have the same approach for building our staff team?

When we are recruiting new team members, we should think about how we promote equity, diversity and inclusion through our recruitment process and how we will attract like-minded individuals who are also passionate about creating and developing an inclusive environment for children.

Recruitment vacancy: you should review the content of your job descriptions and adverts to ensure you are using inclusive language. You should also consider whether your adverts are deterring potential candidates by being too specifc or inflexible with the skills or experience you are looking for.

Advertising: there are many formats and platforms to place a job advert, it is important that you consider how you are reaching a broad audience with your adverts to gain as wide a pool of potential candidates as possible. You should also consider the accessibility of your adverts, is the text formating clear, can they be linked to a "text to speak" software for ease of access.

Screening and interview: be mindful of what questions you can and can't ask a potential candidate. You should celebrate the inclusive practices you currenlty have in place, sharing how you value a broad range of team members and in turn how they contribute to an inclusive environment for children. You are able to collect equality, diversity and inclusion data but candidates should not feel this is conditionary of a job offer.

Induction and retention: to ensure your inclusive ethos remains it is vital that new team are inducted effectively to share your values and practices. You should also ensure you have regular one-to-ones with your team to understand how they work best and how you can support them to achieve this in their role. Understanding and supporting your teams strengths and intrests supports building a positive inclusive culture which people wish to be part of.

When an inclusive ethos runs through not only your provision but your hiring practices you will find yourself armed with a team of professionals excited to work together to further your inclusion journey. Each person in your team is unique and brings their own skills and interests to your provision.

When you are recruiting, do you consider how inclusive your advert and job descriptions are? Think about how and where you advertise. Are you ensuring that the audience of your advert reaches as many people as you can? It's easy for us to specify exactly what we want, but you need to ensure that we are not ruling potential candidates out because they feel they are unable to 'fit' the specification. We need to consider what adjustments can be made to the area a potential candidate could work in and also be proud to celebrate these within your interview process. A candidate feeling that they are already valued could lead to a better outcome of reducing the vacancies within your setting. It can also support retention, as staff who feel valued tend to settle and remain for a longer period of time. The early years workforce is often fluid, with people frequently moving between roles, and even teams within the same nursery or moving onto new settings. To ensure that your ethos is sustained, you will need all team members to be working to a shared goal of inclusivity. Think about when a new person joins your setting or room; are they aware of the vision? Can they see it in action? What role do you play in supporting that? Inductions are normally carried out by the Manager or Senior member of staff, but anyone can contribute, and again this shows the unique strengths of some staff who can further support new people to jump on board your journey.

When building a new team, it's important to really get to know them; this shouldn't be a formal or box ticking exercise but a relaxed and fun one. There isn't a one-size-fits-all approach to getting to know your team, and utilising their skills and interests will support the development of a truly inclusive team. This also helps with building a great first impression, where at the heart of the setting are the team, the children and their families. This should be reflected within the adverts you place for recruitment, so your potential team members are reading this, researching what you do, and then seeing it in practice, embedded in your environment. Seeing it throughout the journey from start to finish supports retention of staff, as they know they play a key part in an inclusive team. This also encourages a positive approach to supporting the children within the setting which offers the best start for the children who attend.

You can carry out team building activities to learn about them, what makes them unique as well as skills and interests. Think about what questions you could ask and create a getting to know me starter sheet, like in Figure 6.2.

This will also create a team that is happy to work effectively and as a result can support the ongoing challenges that the early years workforce is facing in terms of recruitment and retention. Having a team who can each share and celebrate their uniqueness will enable them to be the best versions of themselves, which fundamentally has a positive impact on their children and the setting as a whole.

When an inclusive ethos runs through not only your provision but your hiring practices, you will find yourself armed with a team of professionals who are excited to work together to further your inclusion journey.

Each person in your team brings their own unique skills and interests which when collectively put together, create your diverse and well-established teams. Pulling on the strengths of everyone can really help with sharing the workload and creating a culture where everyone has a voice to be able to actively play a part in the delivery and planning. This can enable your team to be open to and include the ideas of everyone, which will help keep your entire team motivated and onboard with new concepts and processes that may be brought in.

The inclusive team   77

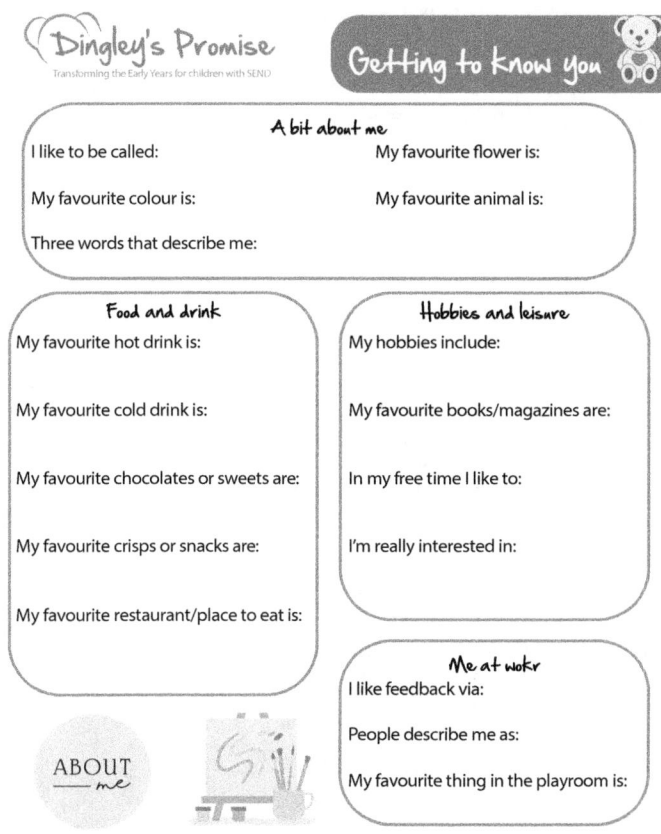

Figure 6.2 Dingley's Promise getting to know your team form example

When it comes to inclusion, it is absolutely critical that you promote and inspire inclusive practice across the entire setting regardless of your role, working with your team to recognise its importance and enable them to share in that vision.

Putting it into practice

When writing or reviewing your job descriptions, you should consider how these represent your setting, the ethos you want to portray, and how you ensure you don't inadvertently deter potential candidates.

Inclusive teams are built on diversity, respect, and equity, and a job description plays a crucial role in signalling these values to potential candidates. To attract a wide range of applicants, it's important that job descriptions are written in clear, inclusive language – avoiding jargon, gender-coded words, or unnecessary requirements that may deter qualified individuals. Emphasising the organisation's commitment to inclusion, such as flexible work policies, employee resource groups, and equitable development opportunities, helps candidates see themselves as a valued part of the team. By being thoughtful in how we present roles, we ensure we're not only reaching a broader, more diverse pool of candidates, but also giving off the right message: that we are an inclusive, welcoming organisation, where everyone has the opportunity to thrive and contribute meaningfully.

Below is an example job description for an early years educator.

Early Years Practitioner – Dingley's Promise, Gloucester

Are you passionate about giving children with SEND the best possible start in life?
If so, we'd love to hear from you!

At **Dingley's Promise Gloucester**, we provide a welcoming, nurturing environment for children aged 0–5 with Special Educational Needs and Disabilities (SEND). Through learning and development driven by play, we help children thrive. We also support families with information and training, and work with mainstream settings to promote inclusive early years education.

About Us

Dingley's Promise has been transforming the lives of children with SEND since 1983. We now run nine specialist early years centres across the UK. At our Gloucester setting, sessions run **from 9:15am to 2:45pm during term time**, with **staff hours of 9:00am to 3:00pm**. There are also opportunities to work up to **nine playscheme days per year** during school holidays.

Your Role as Early Years Practitioner

Reporting to the Centre Manager and Deputy Manager, you will be a key part of our team—helping ensure the smooth day-to-day running of the nursery and delivering high-quality, inclusive care and education.

Key responsibilities include:

- Building strong, trusting relationships with families and making all parents feel valued and supported.
- Acting as a nurturing **Key Person** for a small group of children, using observation, planning and assessment to meet their individual needs.
- Working collaboratively with families, professionals, and the wider team to support each child holistically.

What We're Looking For

We welcome applications from candidates with:

- A **Level 2 or Level 3 qualification in Early Years/Childcare**.
- **Experience or interest in SEND** (desirable, but not essential—training provided).
- A warm, patient, and inclusive approach to childcare.

Why Work With Us?

We care for our team as much as we care for our children and families. Our benefits include:

- Paid sick leave from day one
- Fully funded **DBS check and annual renewal**

How can you get to know a candidate?

Getting to know a candidate requires a mix of direct conversation, observation, and contextual understanding. Think about how you can find out information in a way that enables two-way communication and dialogue, allowing both parties to be able to find out as much as they can to create informed decisions.

Motivation to join you:

- Tell me about yourself.
- What motivated you to apply for this role?

Culture of the setting:

- What type of work environment enables you to thrive?
- What's important to you in a team?
- What does a team mean to you?

How can you enable candidates to really understand your setting and your vision?

It's important to be genuine; don't just talk about the "ideal situation"; be open and honest about the challenges you face as well as the developments that are coming too. All of this helps to understand the journey. Candidates want to see how they'll make an impact in the role and wider team, so it is important to share your vision, values and ethos and build the bigger picture of what it is like to be a child and a team member at your setting. Talking about your vision will support candidates in understanding what you wish to achieve. Inviting them in, where possible, to visit and play will bring what you are saying to life and show them your team in action. It is vital that you show new team members who you are as a setting and what you are striving to achieve, as you want the right people on your journey; and people want to work among like-minded team members. If your ideals or ethos clash or misalign, you may not be the right mix to achieve success.

Conclusion

Building an inclusive team is most effective when inclusive values are built into your processes and approach to supporting children. Teams will have different make-ups and it's important to take time to understand the individuals in a team and how each role overlaps, interacts and complements each other. Knowing the key individuals involved with supporting a child enables you to work together, liaise with other professionals, and develop a holistic approach to support that enables the child and family to thrive.

> **Reflection time**
>
> What does being part of an inclusive team mean to you? How do your expectations align with your colleagues?
>
> How many different teams are you a part of? Do you play the same role in each team, or does it differ?
>
> For children with SEND do you know who is in their team? How do you remember this information and ensure key individuals are involved in the graduated approach and other key support meetings?

References and further reading

Department for Education (2022) *The role of the Early Years Special Educational Needs Coordinator* [Available at: https://www.gov.uk/government/publications/early-years-level-3-senco].

Dingley's Promise (2024) "Dingley's Promise Part 3: Partnerships and Collaborative Working." *Childcare Works* [Available at: https://childcareworks.org.uk/dingleys-promise-part-3-partnerships-and-collaborative-working/].

Murphy, K (2022) *A Guide to SEND in the Early Years: Supporting Children with Special Educational Needs and Disabilities*. London, Bloomsbury.

7
Family partnerships

Megan Harper

> **KEY DEFINITIONS**
>
> Parents/carers/family: The range of adults and siblings who are close to the child. Remember each family set-up will be unique and it is important to understand who is important in a child's life, whether because they live together, they have parental responsibility or they visit or look after them on a regular basis.
>
> Challenging conversations: These are times when educators need to share sensitive information with a family but are unsure how they may respond.
>
> Jargon: Words or expressions related to early years or SEND that educators are comfortable with but may not be simple for families to understand

Introduction

This chapter will look closely at how you as an educator and your setting can work with families directly, providing a holistic approach to supporting both the child and their family. This includes consistent strategies between home and setting, helping them to navigate often confusing and lengthy processes and empowering them to advocate for their child.

As an early years educator, you may be a family's first or only point of contact, and you are often the professional a family will see most frequently. Therefore, you can have the most influence on how a family feels and are likely to be having initial conversations with them when a need is identified.

In the early years, families of children with SEND, or those awaiting diagnosis, are often having to manage an incredible amount of new information and may be coming to terms with living their life in a way they had not expected. Depending on each family's situation, they may have other contributing factors that can provide additional challenges and might look to you for various kinds of support, including practical, physical and emotional.

This chapter will also explore our communication skills as well as how to manage both planned and unplanned conversations. It introduces critical skills in planning and managing discussions, so that educators feel more confident and knowledgeable to have supportive conversations, even when they may be dealing with difficult topics. It underlines the need to use celebratory language and ensure that a deficit approach does not creep into conversations with families, recognising the influence we have over how parents feel in the earliest years. It will also explore theory and research, whilst sharing practical solutions and best practice guidance to help you support families in the most effective way, enabling you to be a consistent champion for any child in your care, especially those with SEND.

Understanding each families own personal experiences

As you get to know each family in your setting, before you can make any informed decisions about a child's needs you must take time to get to know that family and their own personal experiences. There are several life experiences that can impact families of children with SEND and may impact how you provide support to each family.

Understanding each family's personal experiences and additional influences and we can use a framework called intersectionality to understand how different aspects of a person's identity, such as race, gender, class and disability, overlap and interact to create unique forms of discrimination, privilege and experience. We will learn more about intersections in "Chapter 8: Intersections of inclusion".

Whatever you learn about your families as they settle into your setting, take a celebratory approach to children's learning and development whilst supporting the family holistically, in a non-judgemental and consistent way. To best support children with special educational needs, a joined-up approach between home and the setting is best. As we have explored, SEND itself can increase stress in a family home, and there are a number of contributing experiences that can raise this stress even further. You can ease some of these challenges for your families by being calm and responsive to their needs, and this will have a positive impact on the child and their family.

Being mindful of the whole family

When taking a holistic view to supporting a child's family, it is always sensible to consider any siblings in the home environment. In households where children with SEND have siblings who do not have SEND of their own, this can present its own challenges.

It is important to recognise that this is no one's fault, but when one child has higher and more demanding needs, they are understandably going to need a lot of parental energy and attention. What is important is to recognise this and be professionally curious about siblings – even if they don't attend your setting.

"Glass children" describes a typically healthy sibling in a family with a disabled child or child with special needs. The term has been around for a number of years, but it is challenging to identify who first recognised it. Alicia Maples shone a light on recognising glass children in her TEDx Talk back in 2010, bravely sharing her own story as a sibling of a brother with autism and another brother with a terminal illness.

Research has further proven that siblings of children with chronic illnesses or disabilities transform themselves to be what their families need them to be. (Dixon, Deavin & Greasley, 2018).

Some siblings may feel isolated or adopt certain behaviours to appear "fine". These may include:

- Being unable or unwilling to express their own personal needs or prioritise them.
- Not sharing how they feel and labelling everything as "fine".
- Being a chronic people pleaser, being overly helpful in situations and trying to help take care of the family.
- Appearing to be "grown up" beyond their years and talking about family life in a way that suggests they don't experience childhood – taking on a parental role.
- Perfectionism.
- Hyper-independence.

Supporting the whole family

Have conversations with the whole family. Be sure to check in with siblings if they are collecting with their parent and/or carer one afternoon, be a safe space for them and be on the lookout for an "I'm fine" response. Ask families how they all are. If you are worried about a child's sibling, it is advisable to:

- Host a team around the family meeting – inviting the siblings' school or setting to attend and act on their voice.
- Research what is available in your locality – there are often support groups targeted at siblings of children with SEND.
- Support the family to give the sibling space to find personal interests, achieve their own goals and develop positive self-esteem outside of sibling support, e.g. joining a club.
- Identify a trusted adult in the sibling's life who will be their safe space and the person they are able to talk to in confidence.
- Share resources or games with the family that give them the chance to reconnect with one another, e.g. a board game or resources to create a craft item together.
- If you can, consider offering sessions for the child in your care when their sibling is known to be at home, e.g. a school inset day, facilitating quality time together for the family whilst their child with SEND is being cared for.
- Welcome siblings to setting events and consider how you can include them in your setting (providing your registration allows for this), e.g. sibling holiday play schemes, summer holiday events.

Keeping the family and their child at heart

Parents and/or carers are often the people who know their child best. It is vital that we consider this important role at all times, throughout all support provided for the family. Every conversation and every decision for the child should be made with their family, and information provided to them in a manageable way that is right for them. We often hear from parents and/or carers that one of their biggest challenges is having professionals make decisions without their knowledge. They often feel they are in a system that does a lot of things "to them" rather than "with them".

It is important to recognise that many SEND processes work currently in a deficit model. There is often excessive paperwork and form filling, long wait times and little support for a family whilst they are waiting for appointments. Diagnosis is not the ultimate outcome for a family. It may be nice to have, as it confirms family worries and gives them an explanation as to why life is the way it is for them. However, we need to focus more on the support families are receiving during wait times, to help ensure there are happy outcomes for both children and their families.

Every child (and their family) deserves to feel safe, loved and nurtured – you can be the person to champion them and empower the whole family!

Whether it's a listening ear or help completing referral forms and DLA applications, whatever you do keep the child and their family at the centre of all decisions.

Keeping communication open and transparent

Naturally, the more involved a family is within the setting, the more opportunities for communication will arise. It is important that you lead with open and transparent conversation, whilst being sensitive to the family's needs and experiences. If you have developed a strong relationship with the child and their family, you are likely to have developed good communication with them too.

There are several methods that can be used to increase and improve communication between home and setting.

Home visits enable educators to get to know the child and family. They provide opportunities to build strong partnership relationships and begin to provide opportunities for valuable communication.

Settling-in sessions allow educators to ask further questions about the child and get to know them better. They also provide opportunities for parents to see their child in the setting, understand the routine, and communicate any specific needs their child has, upholding the value of parents and educators being communicative partners.

Stay-and-play sessions provide ongoing, semi-regular and extended time periods for educators and parents to communicate and discuss matters relating to the child or family.

Drop off/pick up provides a short but very regular opportunity for communication and checking in. This snippet is valuable in providing context to how the child has been that day, but can also be fundamental in communicating a need for further support or signposting and further planned discussions.

Scheduled meetings enable lengthier communicative opportunities on a set matter such as target setting or progress monitoring. They give parents and educators, and potentially even other professionals involved with the child, the chance to have more prolonged and in-depth conversations in which a greater amount of information can be transferred and relayed.

Communication diaries allow more in-depth communication about what has happened that day. This means that parents have a better idea of what their child has done, eaten or how they have behaved that day. This is even more important for children with SEND who may not be able to recall their day and allows parents to model and engage in conversations about the day with their child.

Fundraising/community events provide another opportunity for parents to share their thoughts and views, not only regarding their child and provision but also in supporting the setting. This provides a different context and communicative opportunities with a variety of people working with the child and in the setting.

Newsletters are an effective way of communicating core information to a larger number of recipients. This is important in making families feel included and informed about what is happening within the setting.

Online communication (learning journey, email) allows for communication to happen regardless of time constraints. Recipients can read and respond when convenient for them and uphold the value of communication without requiring time sacrifices.

Social media groups/pages can be used to share messages, information and events, and engage parents by utilising something they often already use (this won't be the case for every parent). Remember to consider social media safety and gain the correct parental permissions for use of photographs or information.

One page profiles enable fundamental information to be communicated and recorded about the child. This makes for a smoother settling period for the child if educators are prepared with motivating resources and interests. It is also useful for other educators who may work with the child from time to time.

Family steering/advisory groups are an effective way of including parents and/or carers in decisions around the running of your setting, not only do they give opportunities for them to feel included but also enhancing what the setting is able to do. For example, you may ask the family group to read a new policy to gain their perspective, or you may ask them to plan an upcoming trip. Examples of this type of parental communication are shown in Figure 7.1 and 7.2.

Figure 7.1 Example of creating a family steering or advisory group to engage parents

86 *Early years inclusive practice for children with SEND*

Figure 7.2 Example of social media communication, community events and sharing messages with families

 Case study: how parental engagement supported the family and the child

Child C was unable to access school due to a lack of a suitable space to meet her needs. As a result, the family were referred to Dingley's Promise for additional support. Child C attended stay-and-play sessions at our Dingley's Promise centre with her father. It was during these sessions that he was able to ask questions about his daughters' development and be guided in ways to play with her to support this. Child C took a while to build relationships with new people and could become upset and dysregulated if there was not an adult she was comfortable with in her immediate vicinity. She would avoid eye contact with people she did not know, but would make fleeting eye contact with adults she felt most comfortable with. Through monthly attendance at these 90-minute sessions, the team and her family were able to establish a greater understanding of her communication methods and provide increasing opportunities for Child C to engage with the world around her. Her family have seen an increase in communication, using a wider variety of babble and sounds as well as taking them by the hand to communicate her needs.

Child C's father continues to work closely with our centre team and, with their support, has been able to find other services and support groups which help both Child C and the family. They have built connections with others who are understanding and supportive of their child's differences and are now confident to advocate for the right support and school place for their child.

Having challenging conversations

Any conversation you have with a family needs to be just that – a two-way interaction where both you and the family can share information and what each has noticed about their child's development. It is important that you share what you believe would be helpful and supportive moving forwards. This doesn't mean lowering your aspirations for the child; in fact, by offering inclusive solutions that recognise strengths and differences, you will be giving every child the best possible start to their education.

When planning conversations with families, it is vital that as educators you reflect on all knowledge you have about the family as a whole. If the family speaks English as an additional language, take steps to provide information in meaningful ways that can be understood. If a family is experiencing social or economic challenges, include these areas of discussion in your conversation and outline how you can support the family moving forwards. Be led by the family on what style of communication works best for them and adapt to this if necessary.

Think about your physical environment. Ensure that you have a quiet space to host the conversation, away from others who may be able to hear you speak, or distractions from busy environments. You should also think about the space you are using; take time to ensure a box of tissues is available, add jugs of water and cups and offer families where possible a hot drink whilst you talk. Taking care of basic needs (Maslow's "Hierarchy of Needs") means families will feel in a better position to have a challenging conversation. Providing a comfortable space for families such as the one shown in Figure 7.3, can set the tone for a more relaxed conversation. Often families of children with SEND feel isolated, and someone taking the time in a day to make them a cup of tea and offer them a listening ear can go a long way. There can be a number of barriers that prevent constructive and positive conversations with families, such as time pressure, distractions, interruptions, lack of confidence and a lack of privacy, so before any conversation can be had it is vital that you consider these barriers and what can be done in your setting to overcome them.

Be prepared for your conversation, and ensure you have noted down some questions and considered what the best possible outcome will be from this meeting. If you have videos or photographs to share with families, these can be useful to demonstrate what you are sharing with the family so they can see for themselves. Reflect on your own skills as a communicator; are you more confident in talking or listening? Do you have a tendency to talk too quickly, loudly or quietly?

88 Early years inclusive practice for children with SEND

Figure 7.3 Welcoming space to talk with families

Ensure that the information you share is not impacted by any bias. Our practice is influenced by our life experiences and families' parenting capacity is also influenced by their own life experiences – often referred to in research as "ghosts in the nursery" – this will impact how families receive a challenging conversation in what could be considered a very vulnerable moment for them. "Even among families where the love bonds are stable and strong, the intruders from the parental past may break through the magic circle in an unguarded moment" (Fraiberg, Adelson & Shapiro, 1975). In addition to knowing and empathising with a family's home situation, it is also important that we have an awareness of different parenting approaches and do not make any judgements, even if an approach doesn't align with our own personal values or beliefs.

Styles of parenting

As with any child, the style of parenting they are exposed to will affect their behaviour. It will also impact the effectiveness of any strategies the parents choose or use to support behaviour.

Here are the four styles of parenting generally accepted in child psychology:

Authoritarian: This parent dictates rules for behaviour regardless of their child's ability to follow them. It can lead to low self-esteem if the child experiences repeated failure to satisfy expectations.

Permissive: This parent sets no expectations about what behaviours they will or won't accept. Instead, they try to anticipate their child's needs or underestimate their ability to do things for themselves. It can sometimes be the result of parents slipping into a pattern of excusing behaviours due to their child's SEND rather than seeking appropriate support strategies.

Uninvolved: This parent seems to lack interest in their child and therefore in their behaviour. It is probably seen less often where the child is under 5 years old, perhaps resulting more often from the parent's own feelings of inadequacy in parenting their child over several years. It leads to unhappiness in both parent and child.

Authoritative: This parent can set clear boundaries for behaviour that are developmentally appropriate for their child and consider any SEND. It requires strong self-esteem in the parent but can lead to the child achieving optimum independence at each stage of their development.

By recognising the style/styles of parenting a family chooses, you will be able to offer strategies and support that best suit them. Supporting parenting can present its own challenges, for example, if the family appears to demonstrate a permissive parenting style and their child is struggling with routines and boundaries in setting, if you begin offering authoritarian approaches, you are unlikely to find a support strategy the family will be able to consistently implement.

When you start any challenging conversation, ensure that you meet the family at their level, encourage everyone to sit, and once their basic needs are met and everyone is comfortable, the conversation can begin. For any conversation to be successful, it needs to be a fluent two-way exchange. During your difficult conversations with families (planned or unplanned), emotions on both sides will be heightened, and reactions will be affected by this. Both of you might limit how much information you share, may be guarded in your responses, or feel insecure and be keen to get away. So, you need to make sure you are ready to play your part effectively. This means being aware of the messages you are sending through your body language, checking that you are really listening, and thinking about the words you use. Remember you have had time to prepare for this conversation, and the family has not, so don't take their responses or reactions personally.

Body language accounts for at least 65% of the message we send to another person. Even though our body language can be subtle, other people may subconsciously gain an impression of us through our posture, gestures and facial expressions. Even how you sit in a chair can project a whole range of emotions and messages, from dominance to a lack of confidence. During a difficult conversation, you will also want to watch the person's body language. If they appear to be closed off or anxious, you can try using your own body language to influence theirs and so help them to feel more relaxed or secure. This is called "mirroring" and often happens naturally as a sign of trust or being "in sync" with someone else.

Show the family that you are actively listening to them and genuinely interested in what they have to say. There are several recognised techniques that could be considered to support you in demonstrating active listening skills:

- Asking open-ended questions.
- Summarising what the person has just said so that all parties understand what is meant.
- Reflecting on a word or two.
- Offering careful prompts if a person appears to be hesitant when talking.
- Clarifying what the other person has said to avoid ambiguity.
- Offering short words of encouragement – both verbal or non-verbal cues such as head nodding or "go on".
- Highlighting positives for the family – they may share some difficult circumstances and may need someone to help them see the light during difficult times. It is vital that educators take a celebratory approach. Parents at Dingley's Promise frequently provide feedback that many conversations they have with a range of professionals are negative, based around what their child can't do, so as much as possible it's important to celebrate the successes.
- Reacting – empathise with them, show them that you understand and that you hear what they are saying. Explore options on how to move forward together; as educators we don't need to know all the answers, but by offering to help them and signpost them to the right person can be all the support a family needs in that moment.

Often families can feel their parenting is being judged or challenged when some services recommend or require parenting training as one of the first steps to supporting children with possible SEND. This undermines the family and assumes both that they are not raising their child in the "correct" way, and that more fundamentally they don't know their child.

Be attentive to what you are saying to families and the way in which you are saying it. The circumstances may be different for the conversation you need to have, but the message remains the same – the words that we choose to use, and the way that we say them really matter. In any difficult conversation, we should aim to do no harm. There is a fine line between being honest with families about your concerns and scaring them; between sticking to the message you want to give and lacking empathy; between building or damaging a trusting relationship.

There are some useful things to consider when hosting conversations with families:

- Use of jargon – parents can find this difficult to understand and can also find terminology upsetting. Be aware of how you're phrasing this with them.
- Be aware of the tone of your voice, recognise how you're feeling and how it may impact your voice. Try to ensure you use a softer tone, moderate your pitch and volume of your voice.
- Slow down and meet the needs of the family. Challenging conversations can place families on an emotional rollercoaster. Give them time to process what is being said and time to respond.
- Avoid using phrases that are too woolly; language like this can sound like indecision or a lack of confidence. It is okay to say things with confidence, e.g. "I feel that it's time to refer X".

- Don't give guarantees or promises that cannot be kept. It's not helpful to build family expectations with false promises or absolutes. Be realistic about what you can do and clear about what is within your control.
- Be non-judgemental – give the family a safe space to share with you. Families can only hope to be "good enough" and any judgements about parenting or situations should not be shared. It is important not to let previous knowledge or experiences of the family cloud your judgement in this conversation.
- Try to keep to your professional experiences of SEND rather than your own personal experiences; empathy is helpful, and sharing that you understand an experience, but keep the family's child at the centre of the conversation.
- Ask open-ended questions; this keeps communication flowing and encourages families to open up about their experiences. This will support more in-depth sharing of information and allow you to explore discussion points further.

Sometimes you may find yourself in difficult discussions without having planned to have these. A parent may approach you with a concern or frustration, or an incident or accident may have occurred during the day that you share with them but sparks further lines of discussion. Unplanned conversations can prove challenging; we may find ourselves having to manage families who are upset or angry. In these situations, it's important to keep calm and take a breath. Encourage the family member to join you in a quiet space, providing them with an opportunity to voice how they are feeling in a safe and controlled environment. Where possible, steer the conversation in a similar manner, offer them a drink, a tissue, all those basic things to meet their physical needs. Remember to keep calm, speak in a soft tone and keep voices down, encouraging them to match your tone and volume if they are feeling heightened. Utilising the listening and speaking skills that have been discussed to try and make the conversation productive and the outcome purposeful.

Sometimes you may find that family engagement can be challenging, and although this can lead to professional frustrations, it is important to be mindful of the barriers families can face. Wider issues can get in the way of families seeking out and taking up the support offered by education, health and statutory services.

- A family who shares custody or where there are multiple carers might struggle to consistently engage with support. There could also mean that there is a difference of opinion on how to raise the child or in parenting styles.
- Cultural differences in some communities may mean that professional services are viewed with suspicion or there may be an expectation that family units should be self-sufficient and keep their worries private.
- Language barriers may prevent families from coming forward for help.
- Families may have had previous negative experiences using support services and are therefore reluctant to seek or accept support.
- Professionals sometimes fall into the trap of assuming the family will understand and engage in processes set up with good intentions to support them. Remember, jargon, medical terms and diagnosis can be scary for families.

Reflecting on how and what you do to support families in your setting will help you to identify and overcome any potential barriers. It is important to ask ourselves why a family is not engaging. What changes can be made to approaches, environment and practice to encourage participation? As always, inclusion shouldn't be a one-off event, or an isolated response to one situation, but embedded into everything you do and continuously reflected upon and adapted as necessary. Remember it is important not to judge or make assumptions about your families. Whilst we may have a vision of how we hope families will engage with us, there are many reasons that they may choose not to or may only engage where it is absolutely necessary. This is their choice, and we should continue to keep communication open and offer opportunities to engage when they choose.

Home learning

Children's participation in learning activities, the quality of parent-child interactions, and the availability of learning materials are three key features of the *home learning environment* that help to support children's educational development.

As early years educators, we are in a powerful position to share our knowledge, expertise, and learning experiences with our families so that we can have an impact on home learning. By equipping parents with the necessary knowledge, resources, and support, settings can break down barriers and create an environment where all children, regardless of their family's income or background, have more opportunities to reach their full potential (Education Policy Institute, 2024).

There are a number of ways as educators that you can support home learning for all children, including those with SEND:

- Sharing your curriculum with families and how these learning opportunities can be repeated or extended at home.
- Sharing "how to" guides with families on specific provocations their child has actively taken part in and shown a preference for.
- Sending home meaningful resources with families to explore at home, e.g. playdough recipe card, flour, salt, oil, colouring and tools.
- Sharing song words and favourite nursery rhymes to sing at home.
- Sharing Makaton signs of the week.
- Creating a lending library in your setting so families can choose from a variety of resources and activities to take home and try. This could include different sensory items, e.g. weighted blankets.
- Providing home visits to share ideas and role-model play skills with specific resources.
- Including families in your planning, e.g. asking families to go on an autumn walk to collect natural items such as crunchy leaves and pinecones.
- Hosting parent workshops – create sensory bottles together or heuristic play baskets.
- Using what is available in your setting – if you have a garden area encourage families to help you tend to it and plant vegetables. Work with your setting chef (if you have one)

to plan parent cooking sessions, demonstrate how to use seasonal, home-grown foods or create favourite meals on a budget.
- Using available technology to encourage families to share photographs and videos of children engaging in learning opportunities at home.
- Utilising what is available in your local community and signposting families to these events e.g. Song time and rhyme groups at local libraries.
- Working collaboratively with families to plan next steps and celebrate successes together, e.g. if a child is reluctant to try new foods, the setting could model food play activities and then share this with families to repeat at home.
- Take time to reflect together - what is working well? What could be better? What have the family noticed or felt they have achieved?
- Make it fun! Create challenges or projects that include families e.g. Ask families to record themselves reading a story and then share with children in the session.

The opportunities are limitless.

It is important to recognise that home learning isn't just about the child's environment, but the relationships children have with their family members. Parents are their children's first and primary educators. It is our role to support, encourage and share our knowledge to enhance interactions and home learning environments.

Considering your impact and providing home learning opportunities can be done sustainably and doesn't have to be costly. There are several ways you can use sustainable practices to consider home learning opportunities:

- Many resources can be found naturally in the outdoor environment, leading to seasonally based provocations. Encourage families to go on walks to find a selection of items.
- You could consider what is local to you, such as community groups or local resource centres where you can stock up on donated and recycled materials.
- Your setting could implement a donation list or a "wishing tree" and request donations of items such as flour for playdough.
- Connecting with local shops to receive items that would ordinarily be thrown away.
- Purchasing items, when necessary, from charity shops, car boot sales and recycling/refurbishing centres.
- Asking families to help by utilising their skills e.g. you may have some donated fabric you wish to create lending library bags with, and a family member could be a keen sewer.
- Send home spare milk or leftover cooked meals - offer this to families on a first come, first served basis.
- Connect with local businesses and request donations, e.g. if a local phone shop periodically throws away their sample phones, ask to have them for role-play areas.

Case study: families experience of support provided by their centre

Finding Dingley's has been an absolute "game changer" for this family and their child. Their child attends the centre in Gloucester; she is settled and happy, readily attending. Her needs are able to be met, and the staff know and understand her. The family have noticed an unbelievably positive change in their daughter. Prior to attending Dingley's, they attended a mainstream setting, and their child struggled in a busier environment. She would cry herself to sleep whilst attending and would be dysregulated before they even arrived for their session.

In addition to accessing learning through play sessions at the centre, the family have been supported by the centre family support worker. This support has ensured that the family has always received help and information, and their family support worker will always do their best to help. An example of this is some recent support and information on how to encourage neurodivergent children with brushing their teeth. The family have implemented these strategies at home as their child would never let them put a brush anywhere near their mouth. The family worked through each strategy and whilst some didn't have success, one strategy based on gently massaging their mouth before brushing proved successful! The family are now able to brush their child's top and bottom teeth for 15 seconds each side.

The centre family support worker also created a variety of weekday and weekend events, including a monthly Saturday stay-and-play session. The family and their child have found this session invaluable. Their child prefers being out and about rather than at home and the family found that opportunities in the local community are limited as they often felt judged by other people. By having a Saturday stay-and-play, the whole family can spend time together in an environment where they feel safe and their child can be themselves. These sessions have also provided support to parents as they have given them the opportunity to spend time with other parents who are facing similar issues and challenges as parents of children with SEND.

The family feels heard, valued and respected, and through family support, signposting and events hosted by their centre have been able to "build a village" around them and their family, which has helped them feel more connected with their community.

Conclusion

Family contexts can be vastly different and your approach to each family needs to be tailored to their individual circumstances. By taking a holistic approach, providing them with a safe space, being non-judgemental and offering a listening ear, you can build strong partnerships with each family. Once you have a secure partnership, this will put you in a good position to not only support the family, but manage any challenging conversations and coordinate processes to ensure that each child's needs are met. By utilising your knowledge and skills and introducing ideas that impact home learning, you will be able to help support children to reach their full potential and even increase families' confidence in meeting their child's developmental needs.

Remember to take a celebratory approach with families as too often families of children with SEND feel isolated and in a negative spiral about their circumstances. Too often they hear what their child cannot do or the milestones they haven't achieved are shared. You can be the person that empowers the family to give them the confidence to advocate for their child.

Reflection time

How do you support families to understand their child's needs and make informed decisions?

In what ways do you communicate with families? How do you know this is reaching them and is having the desired impact?

How do you promote learning at home? Are you able to fundraise to create a small library of resources to share with families?

References and further reading

Bowlby, J. (1953). *Childcare and the Grow of Love*. London: Penguin books.

Deavin, A., Greasley, P., & Dixon, C. (2018). Children's Perspectives on Living With a Sibling With a Chronic Illness. *Pediatrics, 142*(2), e20174151. https://doi.org/10.1542/peds.2017-4151.

Department for Education (DfE). (2023). *Development Matters: Non-statutory Curriculum Guidance for the Early Years Foundation Stage*. Available at: https://assets.publishing.service.gov.uk/media/64e6002a20ae890014f26cbc/DfE_Development_Matters_Report_Sep2023.pdf

Education Policy Institute. (2024). The Important of Supporting the Home Learning Environment in the Early Years. Available at: https://epi.org.uk/publications-and-research/the-importance-of-supporting-the-home-learning-environment-in-the-early-years/

Grimmer, T. (2021). *Developing a Loving Pedagogy in the Early Years*. Abingdon, Oxon; New York, NY: Routledge.

Farag, J. (n.d.). A Beginners Guide to: Establishing Meaningful Relationships with Families. *Tapestry Beginners Guides* [Available at: https://tapestry.info/beginners-guides/].

Fraiberg, S., Adelson, E., & Shapiro, V. (1975). Ghosts in the Nursery: A Psychoanalytic Approach to Problems of Impaired Infant-mother Relationships. *Journal of the American Academy of Child Psychiatry*. Available at: https://www.sciencedirect.com/science/article/abs/pii/S0002713809614424

Lehrl, S., Evangelou, M., & Sammons, P. (2020). The Home Learning Environment and its Role in Shaping Children's Educational Development. *School Effectiveness and School Improvement, 31*(1), 1-6. https://doi.org/10.1080/09243453.2020.1693487.

8
Intersections of inclusion

Meggie Fisher

> **KEY DEFINITIONS**
>
> Intersections: Social categories such as class, race, religion, ethnicity, ability, and income, and any other part of a person's identity that shapes their life and the way others treat them.
>
> Intersectionality: The interconnected nature of social categorisations such as race, class, and gender as they apply to a given individual or group, regarded as creating overlapping and interdependent systems of discrimination or disadvantage.
>
> Marginalised: To treat a person or group as insignificant or peripheral.
>
> Discrimination: The unjust or prejudicial treatment of different categories of people, especially on the grounds of ethnicity, age, sex or disability.

Introduction

Intersectionality is the recognition that different aspects of a person's identity (such as race, gender or class) can overlap and create a unique experience of discrimination or privilege. When we consider children with SEND there are some key intersections we should consider: poverty, gender, LGBTQIA+, race and mental health. The term intersectionality was coined by Kimberlé Crenshaw in 1989, referring to the concept of multiple discrimination. Originally, this concept was developed to focus on the double oppression of Black women. For this reason, the classical triad of the concept is race, class and gender, but in fact every category of inequality (e.g. sexuality, age, disability, nationality or religion) can be included. We all belong to multiple groups and that's what makes us who we are. These groups often face differing privilege and discrimination based on historic and outdated views. One person may be part of a number of groups that are discriminated against – for example, being a Black, lesbian, woman may create double and even triple discrimination at times.

Poverty and SEND

There are certain demographics who are more at risk of poverty, with current research showing that nearly 300,000 families with children are living with poverty despite being in fulltime work (Compton, 2024). Disability Rights UK (2024), identified that nearly half of families with a disabled child are living in poverty. There are many reasons a family may be living in poverty, with unemployment and education being amongst the root causes.

A 2018 report by Working Families analysed feedback from 1250 parents of disabled children, the majority of whom were mothers. It found that:

- Three-quarters (76%) had turned down a promotion or accepted a demotion to meet their caring responsibilities.
- Nearly half (45%) are working at a lower skill level than before they had their disabled child.

The report shows that despite taking on lower skill level jobs, parents of disabled children often still struggle to hold down jobs because of a lack of practical support and flexibility. The report found that:

- 86% of parents with disabled children find it "difficult or impossible" to find suitable - often specialist - childcare.
- 82% have trouble finding childcare they can afford.
- 91% of parents of disabled children say finding a job with the right working pattern is a significant barrier to returning to work.
- 81% saying it's a significant barrier to staying in work.

Parents also said they found it difficult to take time off for their children's medical or therapy appointments. The report also showed that:

- 30% of parents of disabled children are not working. By comparison, 26% of all women and 8% of all men with dependent children are not working.

Research shows that one in five families have been turned away from a setting due to their child having SEND (Dingey's Promise, 2023). Even well-meaning settings may reduce or adjust hours with their best intentions to support the child. However, this will impact a parent's ability to work and so reinforce the intersect of SEND and poverty.

Supporting children and their families who are experiencing financial challenges

When considering the financial needs of families, it is important that we:

- Do not to make assumptions about a family's financial position.
- Be aware of local demographics and statistics and ask sensitive questions when getting to know your families.

- Understand the needs of the child and their family and providing meaningful toys and resources in the home.
- Introduce strategies to your setting that will benefit all families, such as a community cupboard stocked with helpful household items (these can be sourced by connecting with local charities and initiatives such as the Hygiene Bank). Connect with your local food bank and register your setting to issue vouchers to families in your care. Explore the use of additional funding sources such as EYPP (Early Years Pupil Premium), DAF (Disability Allowance Fund) and funding provided by your local authority, e.g. inclusion funding or EYMDT (Early Years Multi Disciplinary Team) funding, before adjusting children's timetables/reducing hours. For more information on understanding funding streams to support inclusion, see "Chapter 2: Leadership and management of inclusion".
- Recognise the importance of access to early education and consider ways you can make this as financially accessible as possible.
- Be mindful of the impact of extracurricular activities that families must pay for; this can create a divide between children and their peers if they cannot afford to participate.

Gender and SEND

Children begin to develop the ability to recognise gender at around 2 years of age. By 3 years old, they start to possess a sense of their own gender, being able to recognise their own gender identity between 5 and 6 years of age. Whether we teach children about gender differences or not, children possess an innate ability to recognise differences within their environment and wider community from a young age. It is important to remember that gender identity is more than boy and girl. Within an inclusive society, we recognise and celebrate all genders and identities.

Research into SEND and gender currently focuses on the relationships between boys and girls. Early detection of SEND is vital to provide children with necessary services to support their development, and delayed and missed diagnoses can worsen the challenges faced by children, something which is more common among girls with SEND (Daniel & Wang, 2023).

For example, the National Autistic Society highlights that masking of symptoms can be more common for girls, potentially due to sexism and stereotypes of how girls are expected to behave. Masking is the adoption of certain behaviours, in order to blend in a be more accepted by society; however, this can result in mental and physical exhaustion, low self-esteem and other mental health difficulties, as well as a lack of support due to their needs not being apparent and therefore harder to meet.

Awareness of the differences between girls and boys who need support for special educational needs is crucial, as the point when a child with special educational needs is diagnosed is an important moment in their and their family's lives. It allows education providers and health professionals to give them access to additional resources, such as funding, assistive equipment and technology, specialised teaching programmes or the services of professionals such as educational psychologists. These resources help to meet children's academic, emotional and social needs.

Supporting children and their families with celebrating gender

Children are naturally curious and will ask questions about what they have seen and heard around them. Creating an environment which celebrates genders and showcases people of all genders participating in different roles, responsibilities and experiences, promotes positive and flexible thinking about gender roles.

You might have books which present both genders as positive role models in a variety of jobs such as parents/carers, medicine, teaching, the armed forces, office workers or in science. Having the opportunity to see someone like them achieving a range of career aspirations opens the door for opportunities to explore these themselves.

Don't shy away from questions about gender but do be consistent with your messages across the team – pink can be anyone's favourite colour, rough and tumble or risky play can be experienced by everyone, and clothes don't have a gender.

Being open about gender opportunities, instilling confidence in children and modelling their right to express themselves, freely sets the foundations for them to make informed choices as they grow older and further explore their own gender identity.

It is important for families to feel welcome, accepted and comfortable leaving their child in your care. You should consider the language used in your policies and paperwork to ensure that families feel it is relevant and accepting of them and their child.

LGBTQIA+ and SEND

LGBTQIA+ is an acronym referring to all gender identities, expressions, orientations and variations in sex characteristics that are not cisgender or heterosexual, or don't fit within the male/female biological binary. The acronym covers Lesbian, Gay, Bisexual, Transgender, Queer (or sometimes Questioning), Intersex, Asexual and the +, which is used as an umbrella to represent any other gender identities, expressions, orientations and variations in sexual characteristics.

It is important to allow children the freedom to explore their own identity and for family members to feel confident and accepted however they identify when they are within your setting.

LGBTQIA+ families may be more likely to adopt children, with one in five adoptions being to same-sex couples in 2023, an increase from one in six in 2022 (New Family Social, 2023). Many children who are up for adoption will have been through the care system, having faced adverse childhood experiences. They have an increased likelihood of having social, emotional and mental health issues and behavioural problems compared to their peers, and may have lower attainment in school. According to Adoption UK (2023), 82% of adopted children in England have SEND, which is much higher than the rate of SEND within the general population. With this in mind, it is important to consider the variety of family dynamics that may be present in your setting and to ensure they feel welcome and included.

This can be as simple as checking the language on your paperwork. Where historically your documentation may have referred to mother and father when completing contact details, changing this to parent 1 and parent 2 allows all family dynamics to comfortably complete this.

Research also suggests that autistic individuals are less likely to identify as heterosexual and more likely to identify with a diverse range of sexual orientations than non-autistic individuals (University of Cambridge, 2021). Children may begin exploring their sexual identity from a young age, and it is vital that we support them as they begin to make sense of what they are thinking, feeling, and noticing.

Supporting LGBTQIA+ families

- It is important to think about representation within your setting; are there opportunities for children to see a variety of family dynamics in books and photographs?
- Open and age-appropriate conversation: are you comfortable talking about same-sex marriages and different family dynamics if children have questions?
- Engaging with families, ask families how they currently talk to their child about their own family set-up?
- Be mindful of how children and families may feel at family events; how do you advertise and encourage participation?
- Challenge assumptions or discriminatory behaviours; this can feel daunting, but it is important that we are the voice of inclusion for all, which encompasses ensuring any LGBTQIA+ families or children of these families feel safe and supported.

Race and SEND

Under the Equality Act 2010, race is a protected characteristic, and you must not therefore be discriminated against because of your race. Race can mean your skin colour, or your nationality (including your citizenship). It can also mean your ethnic or national origins, which may not be the same as your current nationality.

Children are forever inquisitive and notice similarities and differences between themselves and those around them. In fact, infants can distinguish between faces of the same race and different races. By the time a child reaches preschool age, they can use race to make choices about whom they want to play with. It is important that as educators we are confident and provide a positive view towards differences, particularly with respect to race.

Historically there have been many inequalities faced by non-white children, stemming from a pseudoscientific belief that Black people and other global majority groups are not as intelligent as White people. Unfortunately, this still has a lingering impact on the recognition and diagnosis of children with SEND, and some may find themselves incorrectly identified as having SEND.

Moreover, children and parents will be aware of how they are perceived by others, sensing low expectations that educators may hold for their success. This is known as double consciousness; the awareness that global majority people have not only of themselves, but also how they might be perceived by others in a society that places whiteness at the pinnacle of the racial hierarchy.

Mental health and SEND

Research shows that 72% of families of children with SEND say their experiences have led to mental ill health and one in five say that isolation related to the situation has led to the break-up of their family life. The SEND process can have a significant and sometimes unrecognised effect on the emotional well-being of parents. All children can present parents with emotional challenges; however, there are often additional ones for parents of children with SEND, who may have to battle to first gain formal recognition of their child's individual needs, and then to gain the support that they need. Parents may or may not be aware, before or at birth, that their child is different, and for many, the first emotional challenge is often around diagnosis. Parents often describe themselves as being under "constant stress", mixed with navigating a situation that they had not envisaged. Mental health issues are often experienced as parents try to negotiate through the challenges of the system whilst adjusting to the 'loss' of the child they had expected.

Many families also experience feelings of anxiety or fear around attending social events with their child, primarily because of concerns around how their child will behave, or how their child's behaviour will be perceived by others in the community. Children with SEND often feel overwhelmed in busy situations. This may be due to sensory differences, limited communication skills or being unable to self-regulate. This often leads to families avoiding social events, further increasing feelings of loneliness and isolation.

Many children may also experience poor mental health as part of, or as well as, having SEND.

Many children with SEND can experience feeling isolated and excluded from their peer group. This may be through their own choice to remove themselves from others as they find social environments challenging and overwhelming, or this may be through exclusion by their peers who treat them differently due to their needs.

Other children with SEND may have challenges understanding and navigating their emotions and, as a result develop unhealthy coping mechanisms such as self-harm and negative thoughts. For young children, this may present as hair pulling, head banging or pinching/biting themselves and is just as harmful as potential self-harm in older children. Children's negative thinking can also be increased by bullying from peers and also through hearing negative conversations about themselves.

Some children may face eating disorders due to restrictive diets related to sensory challenges, other SEND needs, or late transition to solid foods due to medical needs.

It is vital that we take the time to understand mental health in young children and consider how other factors in their lives may be contributing to their mental health and well-being. For more information on well-being, see "Chapter 12: Well-being in early years".

Supporting children and their families who are facing mental health challenges

When considering the mental health needs of a family, your role needs to be nurturing and supportive. You aren't going to be able to solve every problem for them, but you can be on hand to listen, signpost for advice, and offer help where you can. Parents and/or carers often just need a space to feel heard. They are often so focused on their child that they may not even recognise their own mental health needs. You can support parents and/or carers by:

- Taking a gentle, empathetic approach to build their confidence and self-esteem.
- Giving them time and space to decompress.
- Being aware of potential heartache and confusion, sometimes referred to as "living grief", that families may be experiencing and support parents to understand that it's okay to feel the way they do.
- Making a connection – not only between you and parents or carers, but parents and carers all together. Give them opportunities to talk together, meet one another, and facilitate mutually supportive relationships through coffee mornings, well-being walks and meet and greet sessions.
- Knowing what is available in your local area in terms of external support.
- Exploring emotions with children using stories, puppets and props.
- Considering the child's mental health when planning their support. Think about what additional challenges they may face and discuss ways to navigate these.
- Creating an environment where children are encouraged to express their emotions, share their feelings, and are supported by channelling this in safe ways.

Conclusion

There are many intersections with SEND, and this chapter has covered the main ones. It is vital that we remain aware of the possibilities and open to the conversation, to ensure that we are providing the support wanted and needed by the families in our care. Intersections may be present for the children themselves or part of their wider family. It is important we recognise the possibility of these, as well as ask pertinent questions to develop our wider understanding of each child and family. We cannot assume we know what each family is facing, and we should foster strong relationships so that we create a safe space for parents and carers to share their wants, needs and challenges, in order for us to better support and signpost them to the appropriate services.

At whatever point you are in contact with a child and their family, your knowledge and awareness of child development can provide key insights into what support a child may need. There are many intersections with SEND that may present as developmental differences, and it is important that we recognise not just the need to support the child, but also to maintain a healthy curiosity to completely understand the child as a whole and not just through the lens of SEND. Some challenges such as English as an additional language may present similarly to communication and interaction needs, but if they were to be assessed in their home language, there wouldn't be a difference between them and their peers. It is still important to provide support to the child to understand the language spoken around them, but we should also know the importance of valuing and promoting their home culture. Early years educators play a key role in recognising that differences in development can be for a range of reasons, and guiding children and families both to identify and support both SEND and non SEND related needs.

> **Reflection time**
>
> It is important that we recognise the potential challenges families may be facing, but don't make assumptions about our families and their lives.
> How do you gather information on families' lived experiences?
> How do you create an environment where families feel comfortable sharing the challenges they are facing? What improvements could you make to show all families that they are heard?

References and further reading

Compton, J. Action for Children (2024): Barriers to work: Why are 300,000 families in full-time work still in poverty?https://media.actionforchildren.org.uk/documents/Low-income_families_in_full-time_work_February_2024.pdf

Crenshaw, K. (1989) 'Demarginalizing the Intersection of Race and Sex: A Black Feminist Critique of Antidiscrimination Doctrine, Feminist theory and Antiracist Politics'. *University of Chicago Legal Forum:* Vol. 1989. Iss. 1 [Available at: http://chicagounbound.uchicago.edu/uclf/vol1989/iss1/8].

Daniel, J. and Wang, H. (2023): Gender differences in special educational needs identification. [Available at: https://bera-journals.onlinelibrary.wiley.com/doi/full/10.1002/rev3.3437].

Disability Rights UK. (2024) *Nearly Half of Families With a Disabled Child Living in Poverty* [Available at: https://www.disabilityrightsuk.org/news/nearly-half-families-disabled-child-living-poverty].

Diverse History UK. (n.d.) 'A Beginners Guide to: LGBTQ+ Inclusion'. *Tapestry Beginners Guides* [Available at: https://tapestry.info/beginners-guides/].

Farah, W. (n.d.) 'A Beginners Guide to: Intersectionality'. *Tapestry Beginners Guides* [Available at: https://tapestry.info/beginners-guides/].

https://www.autism.org.uk/advice-and-guidance/topics/behaviour/masking.

New Family Social. (2023) *1 in 5 Adoptions in England to Same-sex Couples* [Available at: https://newfamilysocial.org.uk/General-News/13281613].

Pemberton, L. (n.d.) 'A Beginners Guide to: Anti-Racism'. *Tapestry Beginners Guides* [Available at: https://tapestry.info/beginners-guides/].

Turner, E., & Hutchinson, J. (2024) 'Professional Love and Belonging: Anti-Racist Practice with Liz Pemberton'. *Mind the Gap: Making Education Work Across the Globe* [Available at: https://open.spotify.com/episode/7FKElfqqFbNKzQpy9raS2K?si=SURcKuSKRxeEfmlu1fwTNQ].

Wheeler, R., Agyepong, A., Benhura, C., Martin, M., & Peter, M. (2024) *Accessing Special Educational Needs and Disabilities (SEND) Provision for Black and Mixed Black Heritage Children: Lived Experiences from Parents and Professionals Living in South London.* Global Black Maternal Health. [Available at: https://www.blackchildsend.com/_files/ugd/6e0914_096b4feb22b84593bf7db08f3c23ef26.pdf].

9
Enabling environments

Megan Harper

> **KEY DEFINITIONS**
>
> Enabling environment: A space with the appropriate adjustments or adaptations to ensure your provision (activity, resources or learning objectives) are able to be accessed by children with a variety of needs.

Introduction

This chapter will explore different aspects and share ideas to consider when creating your inclusive environment, including considerations to physical, learning, communication and sensory environments. It will recommend ways that you can reflect upon and review your environment to ensure that it remains the right space for the children who are with you at any one time. It will explore sensory considerations and ways to adapt the environment to help children with sensory needs to regulate, feel safe and thrive. It will also refer to some of the environment-based aspects of Ordinarily Available Provision (OAP) and reasonable adjustments.

In the Early Years Foundation Stage (EYFS) Framework, the enabling environment is outlined as one of the four guiding principles which should shape practice in early years settings.

> Children learn and develop well in enabling environments, in which their experiences respond to their individual needs and there is a strong partnership between educators and parents and/or carers.

To create an enabling environment, you need to ensure that the play space:

- Allows children to freely explore.
- Incorporates consistent and frequent sensory stimulation.
- Gives children appropriate challenges and supports risky play.

- Supports children's holistic development, helping them to feel safe enough to explore, play and learn.

Establishing an enabling environment

Inclusive practice is fundamental to creating an environment in which all children are able to engage and thrive. A whole team approach and commitment to inclusion is key to ensuring that this happens. You should consider the vision and leadership of a setting, the role of educators, the environment that you create and the transitions children experience.

For children with Special Educational Needs and Disabilities (SEND), their environment can have a long-lasting impact upon their feelings of belonging and aspiration. The influence of your provision's ethos and attitudes on their peers and educators is also highly influential. Promoting and supporting inclusion alongside meeting a child's SEND needs has a huge impact on the child's mental health and well-being. It recognises the child's needs and looks at how the environment can be adapted to better include them, rather than how the child should be changed to fit the current environment. This change in mindset opens a world of possibilities for the child, as it promotes their differences as something to be celebrated and accepted rather than a deficit that should be changed.

When it comes to reflecting on your environment, there are a number of strategies available to you to help influence your practice. You should be aware of the Ordinarily Available Provision document in place within your local authority. It is important to familiarise yourself with this document as it sets out a universal set of standards about provision and practice that families expect to see in a setting. When using the OAP to reflect on your setting, you may find that additional adjustments need to be made to either your provision or practice, to better support children with SEND and enable them to participate fully. Changes like these are referred to as 'reasonable adjustments' and apply especially to changes made to support children. You have a legal duty to make reasonable adjustments to meet the needs of children in your setting, as outlined in the Equality Act 2010 and SEND code of practice 2015. For greater detail on OAP and reasonable adjustments, see "Chapter 1: Introduction to inclusive practice".

You may also use an environmental audit to reflect on each area of the room, considering your cohort of children's needs and interests and viewing the space from their perspective. This could be achieved in a team meeting, encouraging staff members to "get down" to children's level and explore spaces. When changes are made you could complete a tracking observation of children to reflect on what areas they are spending the most time in and which areas could be improved. You could also use a floor plan to simply draw out areas in the room you want to establish for the children; this will also enable you to make considerations for access and walkways and ensure the necessary spaces to move within.

106 *Early years inclusive practice for children with SEND*

Supporting physical needs through your environment

Taking careful consideration of your environment will support you in helping children make positive progress with their physical development.

When considering access, you should be mindful of any children who use physical equipment such as standing frames or walking aids. By using a floor plan, you can plot out routes within the room, heights of furniture and widths of door frames. This helps to ensure you have a fully inclusive environment, as shown in Figure 9.1.

Where children are developing their core muscles, it is important to present play opportunities at different heights. This can benefit children who use different mobility equipment to access and engage in the same opportunities as their peers, but also allows children to choose what is more comfortable for them. For example, a sand tray on the floor as well as a raised sand tray will present children with different opportunities to play. Some will be more comfortable sitting or lying, whereas some will take joy in pulling themselves to stand and balancing at the height of the tray, and others may prefer to stand and stretch across. Simply by presenting sand at different heights, you have enabled children with a variety of physical needs to meet these within their play.

Building movement opportunities into your day also creates time for children to explore what their body is capable of and to strengthen and develop physical skills. You can do this by having regular music and movement sessions, speakers or music available for children to choose when they feel like having a dance, encouraging children to roll, crawl or jump to their next destination, and creating obstacle courses so that when children wish to move from one space to another, they have to navigate the obstacles first. These opportunities create chances to move their bodies in different ways but also help to stimulate their physical senses and support the regulation of their bodies needs.

Figure 9.1 Bringing experiences and opportunities to learn to the right height for individual children

Communication in the environment

Whilst reflecting on your play space, it is vital to consider consistent and inclusive communication strategies. It is important to be prepared and not reactive to any child you may need to support, and a total communication approach is considered best practice for all children.

Creating a total communication environment:

- Visual timetable.
- Clearly labelled resources with photographs or symbols.
- Clear repetition.
- Modelling language plus one.
- Choice boards.

These simple yet effective strategies will help to empower all children to have a voice, which in turn will develop their self-confidence and self-esteem. All children thrive within a predictable routine; having a visual timetable of your day will help support children to know what is coming next and feel safe in their environment.

For more communication support strategies, see "Chapter 5: Voice of the child".

Sensory and self-regulation in the environment

All children, at times, need a safe space to retreat to when they are feeling dysregulated. Whilst planning your enabling environment, careful consideration should be given to creating such spaces. They should be easily accessible and ideally away from doorways and walkways to create a quieter area. These spaces do not need to be extravagant (a simple tent will do) and should be designed and kept within the environment. Children should not be removed from their room, as transitions away from the play space can cause further upset.

Children can have a range of sensory needs, and they may seek out sensory experiences to help feel regulated, or avoid sensory experiences that make them feel uncomfortable. Consider whether your current room layout is fully accessible and open, meeting all childrens' needs, see Figure 9.2. To be able to support sensory needs in your environment, it is important to know each of the eight senses:

- **Touch:** Are any objects too heavy or out of reach?
- **Sight:** Is the space providing good visual stimulation without being overpowering? Is it too light or too dark?
- **Sound:** Is the setting too loud or quiet? Are there any sudden or distracting noises?
- **Smell:** Are there any strong smells from cleaning products or foods that children may find distressing or distracting?
- **Taste:** Is there a variety of foods on offer at snack/lunch time which include a range of flavours? Are the children offered familiar foods alongside new ones?

Other senses to consider are:

- **Interoception:** Are staff able to recognise the child's internal senses? For example, is the child hungry, thirsty, tired or in pain?
- **Vestibular:** What experiences and activities are available for children to experience the sense of balance?
- **Proprioceptive:** Are there areas in the setting that the child can freely explore their sense of movement or access a calming area for when they are overwhelmed?

By having an understanding of the eight senses and observing children, you will know if they are seeking or avoiding sensory input.

Supporting self-regulation and sensory needs:

- Calm spaces within the environment.
- Low arousal environment – calm neutral spaces, avoiding excessive use of wall space.
- Calm boxes – three to five items, personal to each child, clearly labelled with photo for independent access.
- Movement breaks.
- Consider the environment's smells, visual stimulation and sounds – is there a strong automatic air freshener that could be unsettling? Are there any lights that flicker or make a sound? Do you hang lots of visual items from your ceiling? Is there a lot of 'visual clutter'?
- Sensory resources – do you have enough resources that help children to bounce, spin and climb high? Could you purchase some silicone chewies to offer to children who continuously put items in their mouth?

Relationships

An enabling environment goes far beyond just the physical room itself; it also includes the relationships we build with children and the power of our play. By creating an enabling environment, you will help foster positive relationships between peers and adults. Positive relationships between staff, children, and families are crucial in creating an enabling emotional environment. These relationships provide the security children need to explore and learn (Scollan & Farini, 2021).

Inclusive spaces are nurturing and supportive of all children (Birth to 5 Matters, 2021). Once your play space is planned, it is down to both the environment and educators to nurture and inspire children in your care. This can be done by recognising their interests and knowing what they are curious about, encouraging awe and wonder, sharing experiences together, and engaging in sustained shared thinking. Children should be encouraged to be independent in their environment, and their success, however small, celebrated together to make their day positive and help them to feel seen, heard, valued and loved. Enabling environments empower children to make choices, take risks, and learn from their experiences. This fosters independence and builds confidence (Bruce, 2021).

Enabling environments 109

A child-centred approach puts the needs, interests, and developmental stages of children at the heart of the learning environment. This approach recognises that children are unique individuals with their own pace of development (Department for Education, 2021).

The power of play

When adults and children share positive relationships and there is a sense of belonging and love in the environment, everyone feels safe and secure. This helps to support powerful interactions and develop play. Play is fundamental to early learning, and by sensitively observing and joining children in their play, adults are in a powerful position to have a significant impact on children's learning and development.

It is important for adults to have a key understanding of patterns of play when observing children and what they can do to best support children's learning. Schematic play is when children are observed to repeat the same actions or ideas in their play. Controversially, these may be the behaviours seen in play that an educator may say "don't move that there" or "sand stays in the sand tray"; however, these patterns of play are inclusive of children's passions and interests and should be encouraged as much as possible.

The indoor and outdoor environment

When planning your environment, you need to carefully consider what areas you want to be organised as part of your continuous provision. These are areas that are freely accessible,

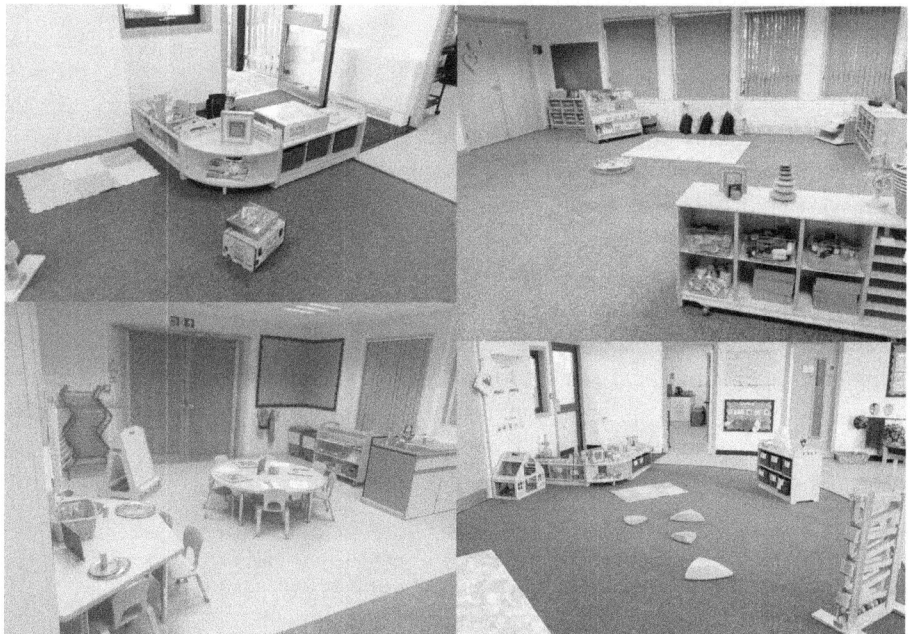

Figure 9.2 Open, accessible and calm approach to the layout of a room

but flexible and support children's ability to engage in different types of play and learning experiences.

Areas you may wish to consider as part of your continuous provision include:

- Calm, cosy area – this could include a quiet reading corner.
- Creative.
- Sensory/messy (including sand and water – will this be inside or outside or in both play spaces)
- Block play.
- Role play.
- Small world.

In addition to each of these areas, carefully consider how literacy, mark-making and mathematics can be woven across all areas, giving children opportunity to develop early skills.

If you are using furniture to position and create distinct areas, ensure that walkways and access areas are wide enough for all children, including those using physical aids. Reflect on the heights and types of resources that will be available and how these are presented. Add labels with clearly written words alongside photographs or symbols. This supports children to be independent and allows children to move freely between areas whilst giving each area a clear purpose.

When resourcing your environment, you should ensure that they are:

- Open-ended to encourage problem-solving and creativity.
- Reflective of inclusivity and diversity.
- Age-appropriate, developmentally suitable and safe.
- Offering a mixture of familiar and novel resources.
- Rotated to maintain interest and challenge.
- Supporting all areas of learning and development.
- Inclusive of natural and recycled materials.

The outdoor environment is just as important as the indoor environment when reflecting on your play spaces and everything available to children. Outdoor learning provides countless opportunities and benefits to children's holistic development. It helps to enhance physical development, support physical and emotional health, encourage cooperation and develop social skills, provide increased opportunities for sensory exploration and support children to develop an awareness of the environment and respect for nature.

There are a number of key benefits of outdoor learning:

- Promoting imagination and creativity.
- Offering space for large-scale play, movement and activities.
- Supporting emotional well-being and helps children regulate.
- Encouraging problem-solving and risk-taking.

Children with SEND can engage in risky play and this supports a number of sensory needs and helps them to feel regulated and to thrive. We may often see children sensory-seeking, climbing on items to gain the feeling of being up high – so give them something safe to climb on. This could be specific equipment, large cable reels or trees – the higher, the better. All children generally feel happier when outside; meeting other children where they are comfortable and sensitively joining their play not only builds relationships, but also supports children's learning and development.

Outdoor play spaces don't need to be extravagant; in fact, natural and organic is often better for children. You don't need to subscribe to expensive training programmes to develop founding principles in your outdoor area. Instead, research what approaches align with your values and beliefs and adapt them to meet the needs of your children. You may wish to draw comparisons on specific approaches and draw upon the knowledge and experience of others to influence your practice and outdoor learning environments. One example of this is Scandinavian Forest Schools. Waite et al. (2015) concluded that whilst there are commonalities between Scandinavian and UK approaches, such as the naturalistic and progressive pedagogy and the holistic and child-centred approach, there are more differences. Scandinavian Forest Schools are summarised as pedagogically bottom-up, part of the curriculum, regular and widespread, led by generalist classroom teachers with safety not a barrier. UK Forest Schools compares as a top-down, elective (with time being limited), led by specialist trained leaders with identified barriers of risk, safety and cost. Research theorists and influences that best align with your own passions and ethos, planning these into your environment in a way that is purposeful for your children. Whatever you choose to do in your setting, do it with confidence and with children at the heart of your decisions.

When designing your outdoor space, consideration should be given to all areas of learning within the EYFS, providing a broad and balanced learning experience and diverse opportunities for children. You should also consider the eight senses and how these can be woven into all areas of opportunity.

Practical elements to consider in your outdoor environment:

- Quiet, sheltered spaces.
- Variety of textures and walking surfaces (grass, bark chips, large pebbles).
- Natural loose parts.
- Growing areas.
- Water play.
- Differentiated heights, levels and gradients.
- Mud kitchen with authentic resources.

Exposure to nature and appropriate risk-taking are crucial for children's development. They build resilience, confidence and physical skills.

It is important to remember that the outdoor environment is not just an "add on" to the indoor environment but an essential part of an overall enabling environment within the EYFS. Figure 9.3 shows the diverse outdoor environment at a Dingley's Promise specialist early years SEND centre. The indoors and outdoors should be used fluidly and mixed together to provide children with rich learning experiences. In the same way you approach your indoor

Figure 9.3 A Dingley's Promise outdoor environment

environment, you should approach your outdoor environment; this includes providing visuals and taking a total communication approach to layout and resources. Providing children with outdoor choice boards and labelling storage sheds with photographs of items inside so they can clearly communicate if they would like to get something out.

Routines and boundaries

All children need routines and boundaries to feel safe in their environment and have an understanding of what is expected of them. It is good practice to implement a visual timetable of your day; this should be broken down into four to five steps at a time and removed as each step of the routine is completed. As children grow in confidence with their routine, they may even begin to interact with the visual timetable, sharing what is coming next and helping key people to change photographs/symbols. By empowering children and giving them confidence in their routine, we can support them to feel safe in their environment. When children feel safe and secure, they are able to explore, interact, and learn.

Whilst predictability is good for children, it's also important to be mindful of having a flexible routine. Sometimes the needs of children, or the hustle and bustle of a busy day mean we have to make small adjustments throughout the day. It's okay if children don't sit down for a snack at exactly 10.30 am. As long as children are safe and happy, be flexible.

As a team, it's important to agree on your "non-negotiable" boundaries within the play space, e.g. children sit at the table to eat snacks. You then model "sitting" and the sign to all children, so they are clear. It's also important to explore the function of any boundaries you may have: why are they in place? Do they have a purpose, or do you shout 'indoor voices' lots of times a day with no real rhyme or reason?

Children need to run; they need to climb, especially when sensory-seeking. Look at your indoor and outdoor environments; decide what is safe to climb and the areas children will be redirected to should they climb a table. Do children have to sit on the carpet with their legs crossed to listen to a story? If a child needs to feel safe to learn, perhaps children could sit a little away from the group, in a space where they are comfortable. If they're standing at the end of the toy shelf looking at the story, then they will be listening far more than they would be if repeatedly told to "sit down on the mat".

Sustainability

Creating enabling environments that support children with SEND doesn't have to be expensive. There are many sustainable methods that can be used to enhance your provision. Recycling, reusing and refurbishing are fantastic ways to develop your environment and a climate action plan can be made to teach children about sustainable practices for their future.

Sustainable ideas that can support your practice:

- Register with your local resource centres – these often have donations of recycled resources, paper, card and other consumables early years settings typically use a lot of.
- Consider loose parts and recycled materials in your environment and how these can be used; for example, cardboard tubes in the block play area, or pinecones in the role play area as open-ended food.
- Make purchases from charity shops and recycling centres – you can find a number of resources.
- Repurpose and upcycle – you could invest in some furniture paint/wax, chalkboard paint and acrylic paint markers. Then you have an upcycling kit that will help create new from old. Utilise resources such as pallets from deliveries and turn them into purposeful items, e.g. a music wall.
- Donation "giving" tree – in your setting, display a giving tree of items you would be grateful to receive; this could include resources like bags of flour for playdough or baking ingredients.
- Utilise outdoor spaces – if you have a garden area, look at creating areas where you can grow your own fruits and vegetables for meals and snacks. You could also create composting areas to reduce food waste. If your outdoor space is smaller, utilise vertical planting on fences and walls. Look to the community and explore green spaces and allotments.
- Invite families to support sustainability – create a gardening group where family members can give their time to tend to the outdoor space – great for connecting families together and improving mental health.
- Create sustainability policies and procedures so your approach is consistent across the setting and staff have clear expectations.
- Weave sustainability into your curriculum, use the natural world to collect objects for activities, read books on the oceans and recycling. Empower children to be environmentally minded.

Conclusion

The environment you create is a powerful tool in promoting inclusion within your setting. It has the potential to limit and exclude when not set up effectively, but equally can provide a space in which all children feel welcome, like they belong and are able to access a variety of learning opportunities alongside their peers. Your environment should be a reflection of inclusive practice as your standard, rather than making changes for each child as they join your setting. This ensures that families feel welcome from the start, children can access learning as soon as they join and your team are able to engage and be in the moment with children rather than reacting and making changes as they realise things don't work for everyone. Remember your environment is both the physical set-up indoors and outdoors, but is also other spaces within your community that you are able to access and the actions and teachings of the educators. Knowing how to support children in the moment, how to direct play and behaviours safely and providing a consistent approach and boundaries is vital to enabling children to thrive in your setting.

Reflection time

When reflecting on your indoor and outdoor environments it's vital to keep children at the centre of any decisions made and areas to be created in purposeful ways that encourage children to explore. As a staff team, you could investigate the play space as if you were the children, get down to their level, interact and engage with resources, see what elements are most and least engaging. Once you've made changes to your play space, you can reflect on these changes through observations of the children responding within the environment and through professional discussion. What areas are receiving the most footfall? What resources are being explored the most? Reflect and make changes based on the changing needs and interests of the children.

It's important that children have consistent routines and boundaries within the play space. When children know what is coming next, they feel safe in their environment and will thrive.

References and further reading

Bradbury, A & Swailes, R (2024) *A Child Centred EYFS*. London, Corwin.

Bruce, T. (2021). *Early childhood education* (5th ed.). Hodder Education. Offers a comprehensive overview of early childhood education theories and practices.

Dingley's Promise (2024) "Dingley's Promise Part 1: Inclusive Practice Creating the Right Environment." *Childcare Works* [Available at: https://childcareworks.org.uk/dingleys-promise-part-1-inclusive-practive-creating-the-right-environment/].

O'Sullivan, J & Corlett, N (2021) *50 Fantastic Ideas for Sustainability*. London, Featherstone.

Scollan, Angela and Federico Farini (2021) "Enabling Children, being enabled by children. Reflection on learning environments." An Leanbh Óg - the OMEP Ireland Journal of Early Childhood Studies, 14.

Waite, S. et al (2015) "Comparing apples and pears?: A conceptual framework for understanding forms of outdoor learning through comparison of English Forest Schools and Danish udeskole."

Warren, C (2025) *Neurodiversity in the Early Years*. London, Routledge.

10
Behaviours that challenge

Abi Preston-Rees

> **KEY DEFINITIONS**
>
> Behaviour: The way that a person behaves in a particular situation or under particular conditions. Some behaviours are instinctive, intuitive, or involuntary. Other behaviours are the result of a decision-making process in the brain.
> Trigger: An event, stimulus or situation which causes emotional reactions or specific behaviours.
> Fight/flight/freeze/fawn/flop response: How the body responds to perceived threats, danger and stressful situations.

Introduction

All children express themselves through actions which at times can feel challenging to us as early years educators. It is our job as trusted adults to build safe, secure relationships with the children in our care, so that they feel comfortable to communicate with us how they are feeling. This is not always easy for children, especially those with SEND, so it is important that we understand the different influences on behaviour and how we can adapt what we do, and the support that we give to limit the occasions that a child resorts to behaviours which are challenging. With a focus on inclusion, we must consider how we can support each child and ensure that behaviours don't become a reason for them to not be able to access the setting or the full learning experience.

Influences on behaviour: why we do it

Things happen to all of us every day that cause us to react in certain ways, and how we behave in response to any situation is influenced by four things:

- **The Environment:** Is it familiar? Is it safe? Is it interesting or stimulating? What sensory input do we get from it - Is it noisy, busy, hot etc?

- **Other People:** Are they familiar to us? Can we communicate with them freely? Can we co-regulate by staying in the moment with them?
- **Our Own Emotional Regulation:** Have we shown that we can self-regulate when challenged, or do we go quickly from 0-10? Are we tired, hungry or in pain? Have we been given enough time to process what is happening? Have we got strategies to use to keep us regulated, or do we rely on others to help us?
- **Our Age, Maturity, or Developmental Stage:** Have we got previous experiences that we can draw on to help us understand what's expected of us? Do we have the developmental maturity to meet expectations? Is our brain efficient at understanding and responding to situations? Can we reflect on how we responded and adapt accordingly?

If any of the answers to the questions above are "no", then we are likely to need more help or time to process what is happening. If we are not given this help or time, our emotional capacity to cope will be challenged and we may go into a fight/flight/freeze/fawn or flop response. This is the brain's most basic form of self-protection and communication.

- **Fight:** to face any perceived threat aggressively
- **Flight:** to run away from a threat
- **Freeze:** to be unable ot move or act against a threat
- **Fawn:** to please someone to avoid conflict
- **Flop:** to collapse, become unresponsive or faint in the face of a threat

We must start by considering behaviour and changes in behaviour from the child's perspective. Some causes of a change in behaviour will be apparent to us (e.g. having a favourite activity interrupted), but often there will be triggers that are not so obvious.

To help analyse this, we can use a metaphor first described by American psychologist Eric Schopler in 1995 – they refer to behaviour as an iceberg. Only part of an iceberg is visible to us, and the rest is under the waterline and so out of sight as reflected in Figure 10.1.

To use the iceberg metaphor for behaviour analysis, you can record the observed behaviours (e.g. crying, biting, screaming, etc.) at the top, making sure that you remain factual. You can then consider what you know about the child and use this to help you identify any possible underlying causes for the behaviour (e.g. pre-verbal, sensory sensitivities, home life, adverse childhood experiences, reactions to change) and record this at the bottom.

This process should help you to recognise the function or intent of the behaviour – the reasons why it is happening. Once you have some ideas, you should find it easier to identify strategies which may help to limit or prevent the behaviour from happening again.

Some behaviours are instinctive and involuntary; we do them every day without thinking about it. Other behaviours are the result of a decision-making process in the brain. These actions are the types of behaviour we are referring to when we use the word "behaviour". They can be physical, such as reaching out to grasp something; verbal, such as answering a question; or emotional, such as laughing. Different areas of our brain are involved in processing and deciding how to respond to situations we find ourselves in, and our brain may decide to use a combination of behaviours in response to any one situation.

As we mature and have more past experiences to draw on, our brains become more efficient at processing information. The parts of our brain that control our impulsive movements and our emotional regulation also mature and become better at dampening down our reactions. A good example of this is the startle reflex that we see in babies, who may

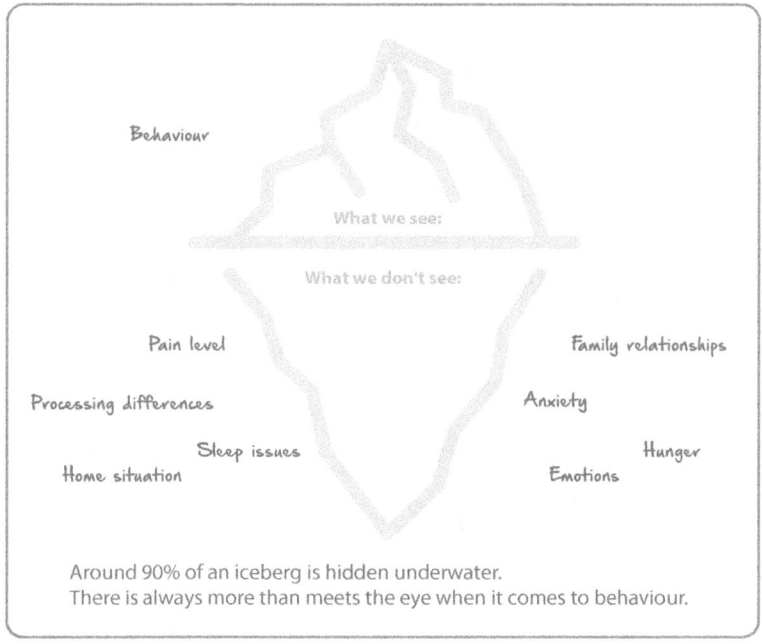

Figure 10.1 Iceberg metaphor graphic

suddenly splay their arms or arch their backs when they hear a noise. This impulsive behaviour usually fades in the first few months of life as the baby matures.

The brain and behaviour

The brain is a complex organ. It is central to our levels of ability and disability in everything we do. Immaturity of development in different areas of the brain due to SEND is likely to lead to us seeing a child behaving in atypical or unconventional ways.

Figure 10.2 helps give us some understanding of which parts of the brain are involved in different behaviours (including sensory processing and emotions).

Research shows that our behaviour isn't just controlled by the efficiency of each separate area of the brain, but also how well the areas connect with each other. When there are problems with the connectivity, this may explain why some children appear to have the maturity to behave in a certain way, but when challenged, struggle to do so.

Children with sensory processing differences (SPD) may have altered pathways for brain connectivity, compared to typically developing children. These differences cause challenges with auditory and tactile processing and can result in hypersensitivity to sound, sight and touch. This can lead to children expressing behaviours which seem immature or different to those of their peers, and they may interpret and learn in an altered way. Attention skills can also be affected, impacting the learning of new skills, and difficulties with emotional regulation can impact social skills.

The brains of people with attention deficit hyperactivity disorder (ADHD) mature much later than those without the condition. The growth of connections between key brain

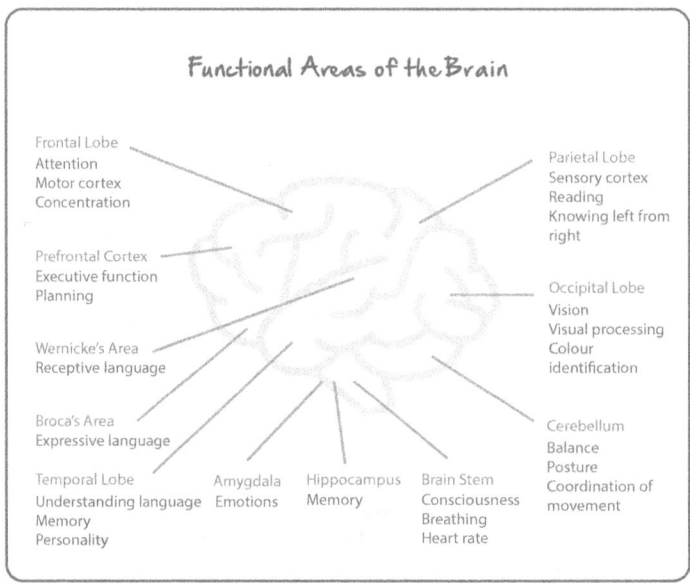

Figure 10.2 Functional areas of the brain graphic

networks falls behind what happens in neurotypical children of the same age. This means that the brain connections which normally help children to focus and control their behaviours aren't as developed. The default network, which is responsible for our stream of consciousness or daydreaming, is particularly immature in children with ADHD. This normally turns on when we are not actively engaged in something and turns off when we are busy and focused. Without being able to turn this on and off, the daydreaming network interrupts the areas of the brain working on tasks, causing children to lose concentration. This may then appear as if they are being disruptive and could be interpreted as a challenging behaviour.

An autistic brain is thought to have multiple interconnected brain regions affected, resulting in differences with social communication and interaction, repetitive behaviours and specific and sometimes intense interests. Some research has shown that there is greater functional connectivity in the brains of autistic children in comparison to those of typically developing children. Whilst other research has suggested that connections between some brain regions are weaker. As Autism Spectrum Disorder is such a broad spectrum, there is much research to be done to fully understand the brain and how the connections influence behaviours; but it is clear that brain differences can lead to multiple, varying characteristics and can mean that autistic children or other neurodivergent conditions have different ways of learning, interacting, moving and paying attention.

Early years brain development in various areas usually follows similar curves. Typically, children without SEND will develop the same broad range of skills as their peers across any given time, which is why we can notice developmental milestones. However, don't forget that by using your knowledge of child development plus your skills and experience, you may be able to identify children who are not yet on your SEND register, but who may benefit from additional support or alternative strategies.

Children who develop according to a typical pattern should respond to age-appropriate strategies when learning to regulate their own behaviour. Most children start to achieve a consistency in emotional self-regulation by the age of 4-5 years. However, this may not be true for children with SEND.

This table identifies some common features:

Development profile	Pattern of development	Typical example	Behaviour support
Overall slow development	All areas follow a typical pattern but milestones take longer to achieve or are never reached.	Global Developmental Delay Down's Syndrome.	Strategies appropriate to developmental stage rather than chronological age.
Impaired development	Some areas significantly delayed or impeded due to developmental condition.	Speech and language delay. Sensory impairment (visual, auditory). Motor disabilities (e.g. Cerebral Palsy, Spina Bifida).	Stage appropriate strategies adapted to meet the need (e.g. visual aids).

Development profile	Pattern of development	Typical example	Behaviour support
Irregular development	Slower or altered development of skills.	Some chromosomal conditions (e.g. Williams syndrome) Other syndromes (e.g. Foetal alcohol syndrome).	Developmental stage appropriate strategies. Recognise the individual needs of the child and be mindful of any condition specific possibilities (e.g. Williams syndrome may need specific danger awareness support).
Inconsistent development	Discrepancies in brain development, some areas mature, some immature. Different pattern of development to neurotypical brains.	Neurodivergent conditions (e.g. autism, ADHD).	Individualised strategies taking developmental stage and understanding into consideration.

Although this is a helpful starting point for interpreting behaviour and choosing support strategies, all children are unique. One autistic child may be generally developing in line with their peers, whilst for another their differences in development may be part of a bigger picture of learning difficulties. Similarly, a child with a chromosomal syndrome may appear to be maintaining pace with their peers until the developmental gap suddenly widens as their peers reach a faster pace of typical development.

There may be some aspects of a child's SEND that act as a barrier to them responding to mainstream behaviour strategies. It is important to gather information about the child and their needs when deciding which behaviour strategies to use. Don't forget that not all children will have their needs identified yet, so you will need to be open to considering all possibilities for any child whose behaviour presents as "different".

For example:

- The child may not yet have the emotional understanding that would lead them to act within typical social behaviour.
- They may not yet understand or realise that their behaviour can emotionally impact or physically harm others and so may not adjust their behaviour accordingly.
- The child may enjoy the consequences of their behaviour. For example, they may be fascinated by the noise or commotion caused by disruptive behaviour, or may want to be taken away from a situation they are finding stressful.
- They may not yet have the social understanding or desire to imitate other children's behaviour, and do not take cues from others during group activities.
- The fight/flight response may be easily triggered in the child, causing spontaneous, impulsive reactions to stressful situations.
- The usual motivators may be ineffectual and reward systems may not be understood.

A consistent approach to behaviour

To choose the best strategy to support behaviour, you must first be sure that you know as much about the child as possible. Collect all the information and reflect on what it tells you about the child. Can you spot some reasons for their behaviour in certain situations? Will that change the approach you have been using? Even small changes to the environment, to how you communicate with the child, or to your expectations could improve their ability to regulate their response to otherwise challenging situations.

There are lots of tools available to help you reflect on a child's behaviour. Here are just two examples:

The **TRUST** tool

Trigger: Consider the impact from a range of stimuli: environmental, sensory, level of demand, transitions, trauma, anxiety.

Response: How did the child respond to the trigger? What does dysregulation look like for that child?

Understand the need: Why did this behaviour occur? What is the unmet need? What are they trying to communicate?

Support required: What support does the child need from you at this time to regulate?

Time to reflect: What can you and the team reflect on to remove potential triggers? What support might the child need going forward? What do the team need to know about the child to support them further?

> **Putting this into practice**
>
> *An incident occurs within your setting where a child pushes another away from them, becomes visibly upset and avoids coming in from the garden when asked. Using the TRUST tool you can identify how you can better support them in the future.*
>
> | | |
> |---|---|
> | Trigger | All children had just been asked to tidy up in the garden and come inside. Children playing near Child R began picking up her sand toys to put them away. |
> | Response | Child R pushed a child who was putting away the buckets, shouted for them to stop and then moved away from the garden door. |
> | Understand | Child R was invested in her play creating with the sand. Child R felt rushed to finish her play by adult and other children. She didn't understand why she had to stop what she was doing and didn't know what to expect next. |
> | Support | Key person to be with child R, use comfort objects to encourage regulating and responding to adult request. Sing we are going inside song to support transitioning inside and offer indoor sand tray with timer before moving onto required activity indoors. |
> | Time to reflect | Ensure transitions are necessary, consider why we are asking children to stop before doing so. (If not hygiene, health and safety or mealtimes does it need to happen?) |
> | | Key person or buddy to go to Child R to communicate a transition, on their level, use visual of now and next or use sand timer to count down to transition. |

Another behaviour reflection tool is the STAR approach

To use the STAR approach, shown in Figure 10.3, think about:

Setting: The environment or situation in which the behaviour happened.
Triggers: Was there anything that might have provoked the child to behave in that way? Include external and internal factors in your considerations.
Action: Keep this factual; what did the child do?
Result: What was the result of their action?

Setting	Trigger	Action	Result	Notes
Lunchtime – all the children were sitting having lunch at shared tables. Amaia was running around the room.	A staff member told Amaia it was time to eat lunch and showed them their lunchbox which was on the table.	Amaia picked up the lunchbox and threw it across the room. They then reached for other items on the table (cups, cutlery) and began throwing these. They were smiling whilst doing this.	Amaia was asked to stop and was given the choice of lunch or garden. They chose garden. Whilst out there a staff member allowed Amaia to run around and climb. They soon became calm and indicated that they wanted to go back inside. They then sat for lunch on a separate table.	Lunchtimes are a common trigger – is there another way we could present the food?

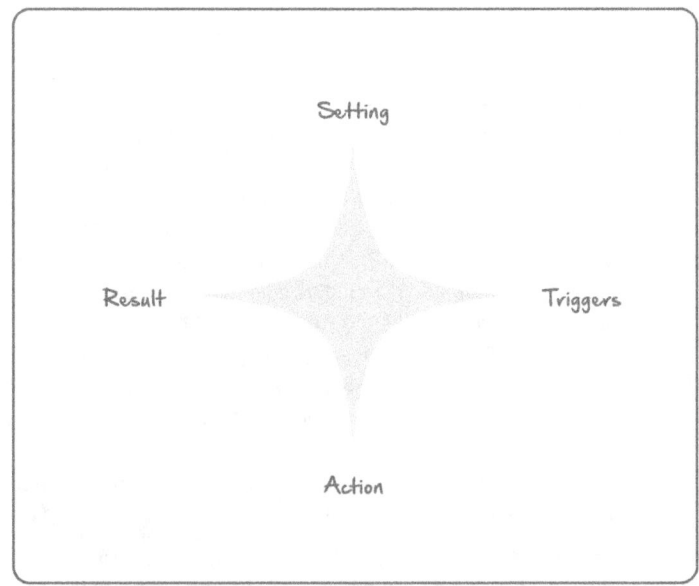

Figure 10.3 STAR approach graphic

Once you have reflected on the behaviour a child is showing and discovered all that you can about them, you can set out clear strategies of support so that all who support the child are able to navigate triggers and implement support to keep the child regulated. This will need to be regularly reviewed and adapted as the child develops and matures and should always involve the whole team around the child, including parents and other professionals.

On some occasions behaviour may be dangerous for the child or those around them; in these instances, you may have to take immediate action to remove dangers where possible whilst you observe and gather more information to be able to make an informed decision on how best to support the child moving forward. This may look like removing heavy blocks that are being repeatedly thrown; however, it is important that this is a temporary safety measure until you better understand the child and their behaviour, and you should seek to reintroduce these resources as soon as you can, so that all children can continue to benefit from these during their play.

Before introducing specialised or individual strategies for a child, it is first worth considering doing an audit of the pre-existing environment and routines in your setting and considering whether these are set up for the children to succeed to the best of their ability.

Often, it is the small changes that can make a big difference.

Possible factors to consider include:

- What happens when the child first arrives in the setting? Is there a clear welcoming routine that helps the child to feel settled and to understand what is happening?
- How is the staffing organised? Do children get a good balance between working with familiar staff and getting to know new people?
- Is the space well organised? Does each area have a clear purpose? Are drawers and spaces tidy and clearly labelled?
- What is staff interaction like – does the environment feel happy and supportive as well as encouraging independence?
- What is the daily routine? Is there a predictable structure to the day? How are the children made aware of the structure?
- What activities are available to the children? Are they challenging enough? Is there anything that may be preventing a child from being able to fully access an activity?
- What sensory stimulation is the child receiving? For more information on the sensory environment, see "Chapter 9: Enabling environments".

As well as an environmental audit, it may also be worth doing an adult response audit as shown in Figure 10.4. Consider how the adults in the setting currently respond to situations and how these responses could be improved or optimised so that they effectively support and encourage the children in your setting. Some factors to consider include:

Once you have reflected on your setting and approaches and you feel it is now well organised to support and encourage children, but have identified children that you feel need additional support with their behaviour, it is then time to consider individual behaviour support strategies.

124 Early years inclusive practice for children with SEND

Figure 10.4 Adult responses to consider when supporting children with emotional regulation

Whether a child can fluently verbally communicate or whether they are non-verbal, all behaviour is communicating something. For most children, no matter their age or level of development, communicating a need through behaviour is not intentional or pre-planned in any way. A child will often have some level of awareness that they feel unsettled or uncomfortable and will automatically and unintentionally display certain behaviours as a result.

The key to supporting a child displaying distressed behaviour is finding out what they are communicating. You can then provide them with a way to meet this need or give them an alternative, more positive way to communicate it. For example, if a child is banging on the kitchen door, then they may be communicating that they are hungry. You could provide a more positive way to communicate this by encouraging them to use a word, sign or picture.

Implementing a strategy to support a child's regulation of their behaviour may be the key to helping them feel happy and calm in your setting.

Consider the following before setting up a new technique:

- **Talk to the Parents:** Engaging the parents in the process will encourage their involvement and enable them to support their child and you by adopting similar strategies at home.
- **Talk to the Team:** Agreeing with the team that you are all going to try a new behaviour strategy not only helps you to feel supported but also ensures that everyone is using the same technique consistently.

- **Create a Plan:** Before implementing the technique, think about why, what, who, when, where and how:
  Why do we need a new strategy? This must be centred around the child and not focused on adult expectations.
  What strategy are you going to try first?
  Who is responsible for implementing this strategy?
  When might this strategy be needed?
  Where are any tools or visuals used with this strategy going to be kept and how can you get to them quickly?
  How do you carry out the strategy? Make sure everyone is familiar with the technique.
  Always keep in mind why this strategy is important and the difference it may make to the child and the setting.
- **Be Confident:** Even if you feel nervous about trying the new technique, try to act with confidence. If the child sees that you are unsure, they will be unsure too.
- **Give it a Chance:** It can take up to three weeks to create a new habit and these behaviour techniques are essentially helping to create a new habit for both staff and child, so try a technique every day for at least three weeks (or longer if the child isn't in the setting every day) before deciding whether it is effective.
- **Reflect and Review:** After any occurrence of distressed behaviour, it is important to reflect. Reflection offers a chance to talk through what happened in the situation (and a great chance to complete a STAR or TRUST tool) as well as listening to any team member's emotional response or concerns around the situation. Reflecting can also be a great opportunity to review any of the behavioural strategies being used. Try to discuss:
  What parts of the strategy worked well?
  What parts of the strategy need changing or improving?
  What is the team going to do differently next time?

Putting it into practice

Strategies and examples

As the adults supporting a child, it is our job to interpret this behaviour for them, work out where this uncomfortable feeling is coming from and why it is causing them to behave in this way. We should then seek to provide the child with a suitable solution. Sometimes, it can be difficult to work out the cause of a certain behaviour, and if you find that a strategy isn't working, have a look for other strategies and consider whether these may be effective. In challenging situations, you will need to use trial and error or perhaps combine multiple strategies together before seeing an impact.

Here are some examples of common causes of behaviours and possible support strategies:

Behaviour cause – Seeking adult attention

Possible trigger	Examples of attention-seeking behaviours
Lack of understanding of how to gain attention appropriately. Busy environment. Complex home situation.	Hitting/kicking/biting others. Looking towards adults when doing something they believe is "wrong". Smiling/laughing when being told to stop. Seeking adult support/praise more than others.

When a child is displaying attention-seeking behaviour, they may not understand the difference between positive attention (such as praise or friendly interaction) and negative attention (such as being asked to stop doing something that is dangerous or inappropriate), or this difference may not be important to them. It is therefore important to show them that they will receive adult attention for appropriate behaviours.

Strategy 1: regular praise

Make sure that each time the child shows a positive or appropriate behaviour, no matter how short a time they display this behaviour for, that they receive positive praise. This will help to reinforce the positive behaviour and encourage them to repeat it in the future. Praise needs to be specific by explaining what they have done well, and it needs to be immediate – if you wait too long after the positive behaviour has happened, the child will not associate this behaviour with the praise and therefore won't feel motivated to repeat the same behaviour again in the future. To help a child understand praise, ensure you are smiling, have open body language, are using hand gestures, and using visuals to reinforce what you are saying if needed.

Strategy 2: limit attention for unwanted behaviours

Whilst a child is showing inappropriate behaviours to gain attention, try to avoid responding in a way that confirms this is the best way to gain attention and continue to model pro-social behaviours. On occasions where behaviours are considered anti-social and risk harm; this may include minimising verbal communication, quietly moving other children away from the area, or focusing adult attention on the child or staff member at whom the behaviour was targeted, rather than the child themselves. They may initially try even harder to get adult attention, so be prepared for the behaviour to get worse before it gets better. Make sure that another adult is close by so that they can support if things escalate to a point of risk or harm. Praise the child immediately for stopping the unwanted behaviour by sharing back their big emotions, both supporting and validating their feelings, e.g. "Thank you for speaking calmly, I understand that you are upset". Some children will need you to keep your words, gestures, and actions to an absolute minimum. Use the same actions and phrases each time the child repeats the behaviour and try to keep a steady, calm voice and neutral expression. This will help to ensure that the child is receiving as little reaction to their behaviour as possible.

Behaviour cause: sensory needs

Possible trigger	Examples of behaviours linked to trigger
Too much sensory input in the environment (over stimulating). Not enough sensory input in the environment (under stimulating).	Crying, screaming, covering ears/eyes. Hitting/kicking/biting/squeezing selves or others. Climbing. Preference/dislike of tactile activities. Licking/eating/feeling objects.

Behaviour communicating a sensory need is particularly common in autistic children. However, sensory processing differences do exist as a separate need for some children.

Strategy 1: meet their sensory needs

If you believe that a child in your setting may have sensory needs, first spend time observing them to determine exactly what these needs may be. For example, do they cover their ears during song time? Do they often sniff or lick items? Do they enjoy rough play or tight hugs? Promoting a sensory-engaging environment will give them opportunities to express their sensory needs in a safe way whilst being supported through appropriate resources and activities.

This may include:

- Removing overwhelming or overstimulating things from the environment (background music, bright lights, busy display boards).
- Giving them access to a range of sensory toys.
- Offering ear defenders for them to use when the environment is too loud.
- Providing opportunities for running, climbing, jumping and balancing.
- Offering sensory activities to take part in and access throughout the day.
- Setting up a "sensory circuit" (Alerting, Organising, Calming).

Every child is different and what one child loves, another may find overwhelming. Try to offer a wide variety of sensory experiences each day, such as the examples shown in Figure 10.5. An occupational therapist may be asked to assess a child and suggest a "sensory diet". This will include specific activities designed to regulate sensory systems and include physical activities tailored to individual needs.

Behaviour cause: delayed social skills

Possible trigger	Examples of behaviour linked to trigger
• Lack of social understanding or awareness. • Lack of practice interacting with others outside of immediate family. • Adverse Childhood Experiences (ACEs). • Attachment disorders.	• Reluctance to join in group activities. • Becoming withdrawn or stressed when others try to interact. • Lack of awareness or willingness to take turns.

Figure 10.5 Touch-based sensory opportunities

Strategy 1: practice social skills

If a child lacks understanding of social skills, providing regular opportunities for them to learn and practise these skills can be the first step to them effectively interacting with others. It is important to meet the child at their skill level when introducing these skills. Some children may benefit from observing others in social interactions. Removing the pressure for them to actively engage or understand the "rules" of social interaction, will enable them to observe and recognise the benefits and expectations when they do choose to engage with others. For other children, small group or one-to-one time with a key person will build on these skills; a simple activity such as rolling a ball to one another can begin developing turn-taking expectations of interactions. Keep activities short; then, as the child becomes more confident, the timings can be increased. Once they are confidently displaying the social skill with a familiar adult, introduce another familiar adult or child into the activity. Slowly introduce more children and apply the skill to a wider range of activities and situations, until the child is confident. Remember the aim is to support their social skill development and not be focused on the activity at hand, e.g. how well they are rolling the ball. We want to encourage confidence in social skills, communication and having fun, so enjoy the process. It can be particularly beneficial to use the child's special interests and engage in simple interactions through these rather than trying to pull the child into your chosen play. They will feel more comfortable and confident in an area of play they would choose for themselves.

If the child is still finding it difficult to take turns, this may be because they don't know when it will be their turn. Creating a schedule for children to follow may aid understanding. Children like routine, so try to stick to the same schedule where possible. Sand timers or countdowns can be used to help the child understand how long they can play with a toy for and when it will be their turn again next. A "wait" card or picture may support this, as well as using Makaton signs to support spoken language.

Behaviour cause: confusion/uncertainty

Possible trigger	Examples of behaviour linked to trigger
Lack of understanding of social expectations. Routine/structure has changed unexpectantly. Doesn't understand the activity/situation.	Resisting taking part. Becoming upset/angry.

Strategy 1: create clear routines

By creating a clear and predictable daily routine, the child will start to feel less confused and more comforted by the predictability of the routine. If you feel that you can't create a predictable routine for the entire day, try to at least make the child's first hour in the setting, and times such as snack times and lunch times, as repetitive and predictable as possible. Once you have a routine in place, try to keep to it wherever possible as it will help to provide stability for the child. Use visual timetables with images to represent each activity/section of the day, and verbal and visual countdowns to end an activity or event. Using a repetitive song at the start or end of an activity, for example, a "tidy-up" song that is sung to indicate that an activity is now finished and needs to be tidied away, will help children to understand what is expected.

Strategy 2: warn of any change

When a routine or planned activity changes, children who find change challenging need to be given as much warning and emotional support as possible. If there is a planned change, it can be represented through the visual timetable (e.g. an external person is coming in to do a music session). This will help the child understand that it is a planned change and not a mistake or oversight. The child not only needs to understand the change but also needs to emotionally accept it, so calming strategies may help the child in reaching this point of acceptance. If the change is not planned (e.g. there is a fire alarm), try to comfort the child as soon after the change as possible. Give them time and space to process and accept what has taken place, then use the visual timetable to visually represent this change. You may wish to have an "oops" visual symbol prepared to use in these situations.

Strategy 3: social stories

If a child has a suitable level of understanding, they may benefit from a simple social story to explain any change in routine or new activities being introduced. A social story is a simple book written specifically for the child and the situation you would like to teach them about. It uses simple photos and sentences that are at the child's level of understanding to explain what is about to happen. By regularly reading the story with the child, you will increase their understanding and help them feel more emotionally and mentally prepared for the change. You may need a very basic visual social story that is only four or five images to help children who are at their early stages of development process the information.

For example, if a child finds transitioning to snack time difficult, you may initially engage the child in a story about snack time at this time of day. Once they are comfortable with this, you may bring the story to the snack table and read to them here. Next, you would introduce giving them snack whilst still reading the story, and then you may no longer need the story.

Behaviour cause: meeting fundamental needs

Possible trigger	Examples of behaviours linked to trigger
Experiencing physical discomfort/pain.	Upset/angry.
Illness/medication affecting bodily functions.	Incontinence.
Not eating/drinking/sleeping enough.	Lack of concentration.
Lack of interoception.	Changes to normal behaviour.
Changes in weather/temperature.	Overly anxious.

Despite the setting's best efforts in ensuring that all children have enough opportunities to eat, drink, rest and use the toilet throughout the day, some children will have a greater need than others and may communicate this additional need through behaviour. This may be due to their medical background, their diagnosis, their home situation, or their own lack of awareness of their bodily functions (interoception). To support these children, we need to give them a means by which to communicate this need and/or restructure the setting and routine to ensure that this need is being met.

Strategy 1: provide a communication method

If the child is not yet able to verbally express their needs, or they become so stressed that verbal communication becomes difficult for them, it may be worth introducing one word/sign/gesture/picture that they can use to express this need to an adult. When the child is calm and happy, introduce this picture/word/sign to the child. Help them to practise using it and getting the correct response from an adult. Once you feel that the child understands how they can communicate their need, encourage them to use it during times of frustration to get their need met.

Strategy 2: adapt the routine

If you believe a child has an ongoing need for more food, drink, toilet breaks, or rest, it is important that you amend the child's routine to reflect this. This may be a structured amendment, such as allowing the child more regular snack breaks or rest time; or it may be more responsive – for example, offering the child a drink if they are showing signs of stress.

It is important to note that none of the suggested strategies recommend physical restraint or moving and handling. As trusted adults, we must take a hands-off approach to behaviour support.

A physical restraint such as holding a child's arms to stop them hitting, or moving and handling which forcibly moves a child, cannot only cause physical harm to the child but may also escalate their emotional response rather than support them in calming or changing their behaviours. Physical restraints and manual handling should only be used in emergency situations – for example, a child running into a road – and should not be used as a behaviour support technique. Instead consider: encouraging a child to move away from a situation that they are finding stressful before any challenging behaviour occurs; providing calming strategies and support to help prevent harmful behaviours; distracting the child with an alternative activity; moving away any staff or children who may be harmed rather than moving the child themselves; moving away any objects with which the child may harm themselves or others; giving the child space and time to calm in a safe location.

Implementing a behaviour strategy with a child in your setting can lead to better outcomes for the child and those around them. It is important to make sure that any techniques used are done consistently and by all members of staff working with the child. The use of a Behaviour Support Plan can clearly document successful strategies, giving all those involved tools to support an individual child in different situations or emotional states.

A Behaviour Support Plan typically includes:

- How to know that the child is feeling happy and how to support them in staying happy.
- What different situations may trigger a child's behaviour or cause them to be upset, and how you can prevent or reduce the impact of these situations.
- How to know that the child is starting to become distressed and what you can do to help calm them.
- How to know that the child is distressed or upset and what you can do to support them.
- How you will know that a child is starting to calm down and what you can do to support them.

	Calm behaviour	*Known triggers*	*Escalation*	*Crisis behaviour*	*Recovery*
Indicators	Smiley. Babbles. Plays alongside others. Follows instructions with visual support.	Feeling unwell. Too hot. Sudden loud noises. Change in routine. Hungry.	Covering ears with hands. Crying. No interactions.	Throwing objects. Hitting others. Screaming.	Quiet. No eye contact. Takes self to quiet space.
Strategies	Praise positive behaviours. Motivating toys/ activities. Visual timetable. Now and next board.	Remove layers if warm. Ear defenders. Consistent routine. Regular drink/ snack breaks.	Quiet spaces. Distraction. Choice of inside/ garden.	Remove objects from reach. Encourage others to move away. Give space. Offer comfort.	Quiet space away from others. Offer comforter brought in from home.

It is vital that this is shared with all staff involved as well as the family who may be able to implement the same strategies at home.

Case study: supporting behaviours that challenge

T is a 4-year-old child attending our Reading centre. He started with us in January 2024. He has a diagnosis of autism spectrum condition, global developmental delay and a hearing impairment. T experiences significant developmental delays, and his speech is limited to a few single words and gestures. These communication barriers often lead to frustration, which can manifest as behaviours that challenge – including hitting, throwing toys, biting, and resistance to transitioning between activities within the daily routine.

T's parents reported similar behaviours at home and expressed concerns about his safety and inclusion, particularly with the upcoming transition to school. They were eager to work with us to support T's development and behaviour.

Intent

Reduce behaviours that challenge and support a child's emotional regulation and communication.

Implementation

As a team, we discussed and implemented strategies to support T during moments of frustration. For instance, when he displayed a need to hit out, we introduced a cushion as a safe outlet for his emotions. When T exhibited biting behaviours – which sometimes involved pretend biting and could appear threatening – he was redirected to a chewy toy. We also actively named and expressed emotions for him, helping to build his understanding of how he was feeling. Visual supports were used consistently throughout.

To support transitions, T was given plenty of preparation time, using visual cues and consistent routines, that included now/next boards. On occasions when he resisted transitioning to the upstairs playroom from the garden time, he was instead supported to remain in the downstairs playroom. This flexibility avoided triggering his distress and allowed his learning to continue in a space where he felt comfortable and regulated, supported by his key person.

A consistent visual timetable was maintained daily. Alongside this, Makaton was introduced to support T's functional communication. Calm spaces – including a freely accessible sensory room and a sensory den, such as the one shown in Figure 10.6 – were made available, and T was supported with co-regulation techniques by his key person whenever needed.

Impact

Through the consistent use of visuals, Makaton, and access to a calming environment, incidents of dysregulation have significantly reduced. T's ability to communicate improved, helping him better express needs and emotions, which in turn reduced frustration.

T also began to manage transitions between activities more successfully, particularly when supported by a predictable visual routine.

The staff team grew in confidence in responding to behaviours that challenge, embedding consistent, trauma-informed approaches across the setting.

Importantly, T began to engage more positively with his peers, especially during supported interactions in sensory play. His increased ability to self-regulate and communicate meant he was able to access more learning opportunities and form meaningful social connections in his own time and way.

Behaviour in context

How do you decide whether the way someone behaves is "acceptable" or "challenging"? Do you always agree when you talk about it with colleagues, friends or family? Are there some behaviours that are wrong in all circumstances? What about behaviour that is left to our own moral judgement? And maybe some behaviours are just a matter of choice and personality? All behaviour happens in the context of a society or culture, and whether the behaviour is perceived as needing to be stopped will depend on the rules of that group.

When helping a family to support their child's behaviour, you must be aware of the context in which they are raising their child. If some of their opinions or judgements about dealing with behaviour conflict with your own, or those of the setting you work in, you will need to find a way to compromise if you want to be partners in the process.

So, when we think about "challenging behaviour" we should consider whose expectation it is that the behaviour should be stopped. And should we instead be trying to educate society to accept different types of behaviour, and to understand that behaviour that "challenges" society might be more accurately described as "distressed behaviour", better reflecting the reasons it might be happening? Rather than seeing the behaviour as a battle

Figure 10.6 Calm sensory space

that we can win or lose, we should instead see it as a distress flare that needs attention, empathy and support.

Working with the family and agreeing on strategies together will give the best opportunity to support a child's emotional regulation. There are some families that may find this difficult and need additional help to implement them in the home environment. It is important to remember that families may be trying to implement strategies at times of the day when the child is most likely to be struggling due to tiredness, such as early mornings and bedtime. Families can feel disheartened if they see the child achieving better emotional regulation in the setting than at home, so remember to reassure them and encourage them to keep going. It can be hard when family members disagree on how to approach parenting their child, and they may have been through, or still be experiencing, a period of trauma with regards to their child's health or diagnosis, resulting in reluctance to impose behavioural strategies. Having joint meetings to agree on which strategies to use will ensure everyone is working together and will provide the family with support and motivation.

Once you find the strategies that work for the child, and support is in place for the family, not only will things start to get easier, but the setting and the child's home will become happier, more relaxed places where the child can build their self-esteem and begin to thrive.

Conclusion

When we reflect on children's behaviour, it is important that we approach it with an open mind and recognise that behaviour is a method of communication and not children misbehaving simply because they can or want to be challenging. Taking the time to observe and reflect on what behaviour is telling us is the most important step to introducing the right support for each child to navigate their behaviours and emotions. Working together with the child's family and other professionals enables you to build a broader picture of the child's behaviour and other environmental factors in their lives, which may be contributing to their dysregulation. Making sure all who support a child understand their behaviour and the strategies that support the child is vital to providing a consistent approach to behaviour, creating boundaries the child is familiar with and the same set of expectations whoever they are with.

> **Reflection time**
>
> How do you currently observe and reflect on what children's behaviour is telling you?
> Take a look at your environment; how does this support children to be regulated? Are there any unnecessary challenges that may be exacerbating children's behaviours?
> As a team, discuss your expectations for behaviour. Where do these expectations come from, and are there consistent boundaries across all teams?

References and further reading

Iceberg Analysis: Challenging Behaviour Assessment [Available at: https://www.teachertoolkit.co.uk/2017/11/20/intervention-1/].

Sensory Circuits | Children Young People and Families Online Resource [Available at: https://cypf.berkshirehealthcare.nhs.uk/health-and-development/sensory-processing/sensory-circuits/].

Social Stories and Comic Strip Conversations [Available at: https://www.autism.org.uk/advice-and-guidance/topics/communication/communication-tools/social-stories-and-comic-strip-coversations].

11
Transitions for children with SEND

Abi Preston-Rees

> **KEY DEFINITIONS**
>
> Transition: A child's move from one setting or experience to another.

Introduction

Transitions come in many shapes and forms, and children go through multiple transitions each day. This includes things as simple as moving from one activity to another, spending time indoors and outdoors, and travelling between home and setting. They may also experience more significant times of change in their early years, including moving home, getting a new sibling or losing a loved one, or they could be starting a new setting or moving on to school. Each child will react uniquely to these transitions, and varying help will be needed. Where possible, careful planning in advance should take place to support the big changes, taking into account the needs of the child and their family. Where transitions are sudden and unexpected, planning in the moment will be needed to ensure the child does not become overwhelmed, using appropriate support strategies for their current level of understanding. To prepare our children for the varying transitions they will face daily and throughout their lives, it is important to use our time with them to build their resilience, self-esteem and independence.

Effective transitions to school

For some children the transition to a new setting is something they and their families will do easily and with excitement; for others this may take more time, with additional settling sessions, more conversations and smaller steps needed before the child is happy to be left. Transitioning children with Special Educational Needs and Disabilities (SEND) from their early years (EY) setting to school will almost certainly be more complex than the support needed for most other children. They may face challenges of adjustment and adaptation and will need time and planning by adults who know them well to ensure a smooth and effective transition. They may need individual care plans and risk assessments, and school staff may need to be trained in the use of medical equipment, adaptive aids and emergency medication. All effective long-term transitions involve a period of preparation, followed by the actual move or change, and then a process of adjustment and acceptance. This process may take longer for children with SEND, and careful consideration needs to be made to ensure the process is well planned and approached in a collaborative way.

The SEN Code of Practice 2015 (p. 88) states that:

> **Transition 5.47** SEN support should include planning and preparing for transition, before a child moves into another setting or school. This can also include a review of the SEN support being provided or the EHC plan. To support the transition, information should be shared by the current setting with the receiving setting or school. The current setting should agree with parents the information to be shared as part of this planning process.

This emphasises the importance of early preparation and sharing of vital information.

The SEND Code of Practice (6.17) also stresses the importance of preventing a widening of the attainment gap between a child with SEND and their peer group. A big transition to a new school risks a widening of this gap for multiple reasons:

- Lower levels of development, especially in the social and communication skills needed for coping with change, will mean that a child with SEND has a different starting point to their peers. They are likely to work through the stages of transition at a slower pace and so will be ready to start learning later than the other children.
- Gaps in development (especially autistic children) may be disguised by apparent ability or masked by the child copying others, leaving an insecure foundation for later learning.
- The other children are likely to have an intellectual spurt triggered by the transition, showing a rapid expansion of their brain capacity stimulated and sustained by the richer learning environment. This cognitive response may be later in children with SEND.
- Children with SEND may be less able to ask for help or express their needs, and so subtle gaps in understanding may be missed.
- Children with SEND may experience a fall in their self-esteem due to a lower ability to access the curriculum, and immature resilience and persistence. This will impact their ability to cope with the transition and to start moving on in their learning.

Effective transitions between EY settings and school can help minimise the risk of a widening gap in learning. Person-centred planning around the child's needs, partnership working with families and other professionals, and a consistent approach, should all help to ensure that the child gets the best start possible in their new setting, maintains their self-esteem throughout and achieves a sense of belonging in their new school.

When a child with SEND moves from their EY setting to school, every person involved is likely to have their own needs as the transition progresses:

The Child: We often talk about typically developing children "outgrowing" their preschool environment. Their maturity is such that they need new challenges to fulfil their rapid development in ability and learning. A child whose developmental levels are behind their peers may not have the same capacity to cope with such a big change and will need a longer period of preparation and adjustment.

The Parents: Parents of children with SEND are often wary of change and express concerns about whether a larger environment with different staffing ratios will be able to meet the needs of their child. Helping the parents to develop a trusting relationship with the school will be important to the child's own confidence in the procedure.

The Settings: Professionals involved in the child's transition will also need time and preparation for the change. The child's EY keyworker may start to feel an impending sense of loss or be concerned about when the child moves on; and the school teaching staff may feel nervous about their ability to meet the needs of the child amongst the others in the class.

Everyone will have a part to play in making the transition successful. Establishing a plan as early as the autumn term prior to a summer move will help to ensure that reasonable adjustments have been made, staff training has been provided, and where necessary, transport and funding have been agreed. Experience tells us that a successful transition is likely to take at least a year, from the first preparations in the autumn term before the child moves from their EY setting, through to the transfer of the parents' trust in the spring term after the child is established at school.

Looking at the transition from the point of view of the child should always be our starting point when individualising support, whether that be for small daily transitions or moving on to their next education setting. We don't just want to consider what is important *for* the child (visuals, walking aids, hearing aids, medication) but also what is important *to* the child (what and who makes them happy and relieves their worries). For children with SEND, being "ready" for school may not mean having developmentally appropriate skills in reading, writing and speaking. More important for them will be having a sense of optimism about the transition, learning skills of resilience, tolerance and persistence, and being as independent as possible in self-care. Being independent in everyday tasks helps children to cope in a school environment and increases their sense of belonging and is key to maintaining self-esteem. Early Years settings can prepare children for the transition to school by spending time teaching, supporting and practising self-help skills. Being able to do as much as possible for themselves relieves their dependence on adult assistance and often facilitates casual, impromptu social opportunities which are otherwise hampered by adult intervention. Consider where the child's motivation is going to come from to achieve independence in a certain skill, especially as they may have become used to a lot of adult help and may miss the attention that brings. Simple strategies that can be implemented early on to promote independence can include: simple adaptations to the physical environment – e.g. how the furniture is arranged; alternative communication methods – e.g. Makaton; visuals, so that they can ask for help when they need it; developmentally appropriate activities that they can access without support – e.g. always offer sand and water play; independence aids

– e.g. "tissue station", task-sequencing boards; reducing sensory input – e.g. introduce soft furnishings to absorb noise.

Once a child has mastered a self-help skill in one situation, they are likely to need help to generalise that skill. This means that you may have to teach and test the skill in different places, e.g. home and preschool, at different times of the day, and with different resources, e.g. drying hands using a towel and a hand dryer.

As an adult, you understand the context of the transition between EY setting and school. You know why it happens and are familiar with the differences between the two environments. Children have no experience of this particular change and for some of them, it will be their first big change since starting preschool. Whilst some children outgrow their EY setting and have the mental capacity to begin to prepare themselves for the upcoming change, others, and especially those with SEND, are likely to need help. It is important that they develop resilience to cope with the process and understand the benefits of persisting when challenged by a task. These skills are called "learning dispositions" and you can support their development whilst teaching the child the key skills they will need to succeed in their new setting.

You can start by familiarising the children with the concept of change. When done effectively, this can help children to construct memories of successful transitions which you can remind them of if they start to struggle later. Teach them to cope with big changes by creating opportunities to practise dealing with small changes. For example, move the snack table in your setting to a different part of the room, or swap the children's pegs around in the cloakroom. Think about what preparation the child with SEND might need for this and put steps and strategies into place to support them. Evaluate how well they coped and what helped, and then consider next steps. Some of the strategies you could consider using are: social stories, visual timetables such as shown in Figure 11.1, now and next boards, objects of reference. These can be used throughout a child's time with you and will reinforce that transitions, no matter how big or small, are not to be feared.

Figure 11.1 Child and educator engaging in parallel play

As part of ongoing preparation for transition, you could consider capturing the child's voice in a one-page profile. This document captures the essence of the child's character and needs, and acts as a starting point in getting to know them. It isn't designed to replace the reports written by health and educational professionals but should be a representation of the child's own thoughts and views. It is a useful reference and creates a snapshot of the child's likes, dislikes and support needs and helps to instil a sense of belonging for the child.

For a copy of the "one-page profile", see "Chapter 4: Monitoring and assessment".

Strategies that support children with SEND can often be beneficial to their peers as well. To be more inclusive, you may want to consider doing one-page profiles with all children on transition into your setting, and review them when things change, or as an ongoing discussion forum with the family/child that's updated regularly and can go with them to their next education setting.

Children will settle more quickly in a new setting if they feel they fit in and have a sense of belonging. They need to feel comfortable in the environment and accepted and valued by those around them. As recognised by Maslow (1943), it is fundamentally important to our well-being and self-esteem, and in our children it is a necessary basic foundation to being ready and able to learn. In order to feel a strong sense of belonging, we all benefit from having people around us who have the same interests as us, look and behave like us, and an environment that feels welcoming and safe. How might you feel if you looked different, couldn't relate to those around you or found the environment intimidating? All of these things may be true for children with SEND, whether they have physical differences, sensory impairments, are pre-verbal or just enjoy playing alone. It is possible that children with SEND may be aware if there is a sense of concern, or even negativity, towards them from their new setting if it is not fully equipped to support them. Feelings of not belonging are likely to manifest as complex negative emotions. And when we are feeling strong emotions, the logical parts of our brain take a step back to allow room for the emotional response. We may enter a state of "hyper-arousal" and this can lead to us being less able to communicate freely and calmly; less able to take on board what people are telling us (and so to learn); and less likely to respond positively to the world around us.

Navigating barriers to effective transitions

Common barriers to a sense of belonging which might exist for children with SEND include: physically not being able to do things that their peers can do; being the only one who needs medical equipment; being unable to talk in sentences; needing an adult to help with self-care and toileting; not being ready to join in with peers; experiencing sensory overload; taking longer to do everything than their friends.

There are ways to mitigate or remove some of these barriers by introducing the following:

- Have pictures, books and toys that reflect the child's differences in positive ways – e.g. pictures of groups of children that include those with relevant disabilities.
- Centre activities and lessons for all children around the SEND child's abilities so that they are sometimes the best in the class.

- Try to give children who wear nappies as close to the same toileting experience as their friends (when, where, who with, etc.).
- When arranging outings, try to choose venues that don't exaggerate a child's disabilities.
- If the child with SEND sits in a chair for group times, allow all children to sit on chairs.
- Don't over-protect the child with SEND. Allow them to take (supervised) risks and make mistakes like the other children.
- If aspects of the school uniform impact the child's ability to be independent, consider adjusting the uniform requirements for all children.
- Consider the child's needs, especially on "special days". Will they understand why they are wearing their pyjamas to school on fundraising days? Can Sports Day be adapted to be more inclusive?
- Adapt clear and consistent routines as these facilitate independence and relieve anxiety.
- Make sure that you teach children what to do rather than focusing on what they can't or mustn't do.

Once a child with SEND has transitioned from your setting, it can be beneficial to monitor their well-being and progress in learning. Both elements can contribute to your evaluation of how successful the transition process has been for the child. Reflecting on what worked well and what was less successful will help you adjust transitions for future children with SEND. By considering in advance what elements of the transition you want to monitor and how you will measure success, it will be a useful exercise for planning the transition process for the child.

A collaborative approach to transitions

We also need to consider the transition period from the perspective of the child's family as they can make a huge contribution to the success of a transition. It is important to remember that families are unique and complex, and the child may be cared for by a variety of family members, carers and even professionals. Understanding the structure of the child's individual family and the context in which they are being raised will be important to ensure that all significant adults (including non-resident parents), and siblings are included in the process and feel valued.

Parents of children with SEND are often very aware that they can come across as overly anxious and protective of their child. This may become even more prevalent when transitioning their child to a new setting, so building a trusting relationship with them will be vital as they are essential partners during the transition process and will require your support and understanding.

The psychologist Urie Bronfenbrenner's Ecological Systems Theory (1979), recreated in Figure 11.2, can help us to understand the vital role parents and carers can play in the transition process. You can see the five systems in the diagram below, but in the context of EY transitions we only need to be aware of the child, their microsystem (which consists of those people who most directly impact the child and their development), and the

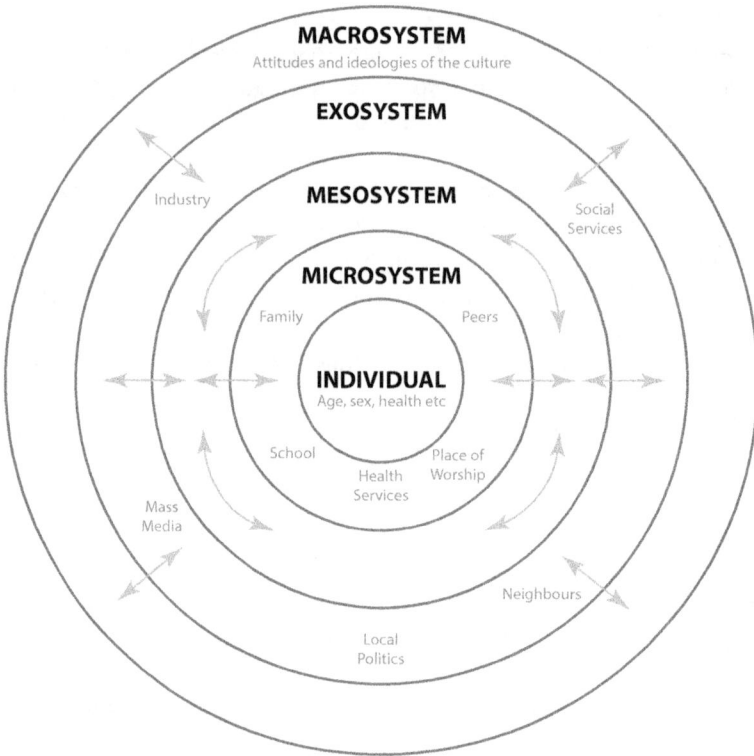

Figure 11.2 Dingley's Promise diagram of Bronfenbrenner's Ecological Systems Theory (1979)

mesosystem. The mesosystem supports interconnections and links between the people in the microsystem, for example between those at school and those at home.

Brofenbrenner suggests that the more links there are in the mesosystem, the better the child is supported and develops. This can also be applied to transitions. Family members link to the child, as well as the EY setting, the school, and other professionals, etc., and so are a constant element in the mesosystem. We can use them and their knowledge of their child to ensure that there are similarities and consistencies between all environments that the child inhabits, and the approaches and strategies used in them.

We know that parents can be unsettled by the prospect of their child starting school, so it is important to make sure they are part of the process. Asking them to make comparisons between the EY setting, the school setting, and the home setting to suggest areas where similarities can be achieved in the environment and in strategies used will be hugely beneficial for all. The parents' involvement at each stage and the changes and strategies they suggest will together form an effective mesosystem, linking all the elements in the child's microsystem and helping to ensure a successful transition. By listening to the family, we can create emotional security which will help to build trust, not just in the process, but also in the future. Their life experiences to date, their culture, their faith and even their financial status will affect how much support they may need as part of the transition process.

When assessing the support a family will need, you should check their understanding of what is happening. You could consider some of the following: Did they themselves go to school locally, or do they need help to understand the system?; Do they understand the importance of getting their child to school every day and on time?; Will they need to use before/after school clubs, and have they talked to these services about their child? Once you have established the areas of need, you will be able to include these within your transition plan and assess what other support may be needed.

When planning how to include families in a child's transition, don't forget about the siblings. Their lives are possibly more entwined with that of their brother or sister than in other sibling relationships. Refer to "Chapter 7: Family partnerships" for more detail on understanding and supporting the role siblings play to a child with SEND. Older siblings may have mixed feelings about their brother or sister transitioning to their own school. Perhaps school for them is a place to be themselves rather than "the sister/brother of ..."; perhaps they are worried that other children will laugh at their sibling or tease them; and perhaps they share some of the anxieties about the child usually associated with a parent such as health worries. On the other hand, siblings can be useful mentors for the child with SEND. They can take a role in the mesosystem acting as a constant in their brother's/sister's life. They might be proud of their sibling and keen to help.

As part of our transition planning, we will need to monitor the well-being of the family with regards to their child and measure the effectiveness of their relationship with the school. As with the child, reflecting on what worked well for the family and what was less successful will not only help inform you of their ongoing support needs but will also help you adjust transitions for future families. The transition plan should be co-produced by staff (from both the EY setting and the school) and the parents. This is crucial in helping the family to understand and own their role in supporting the transition process.

Alongside the family members, we must consider the Team Around the Child (TAC), or the Team Around the Family (TAF), including staff from the early years setting (key person, SENCO) and those in the receiving school, most notably the Class Teacher, Foundation Stage Lead and SENCO. Supporting professionals may also include health staff such as a Speech and Language Therapist or a specialist nurse; education professionals such as an Educational Psychologist, a Portage worker, and a Local Authority SEN team member; and also possibly someone from the Social Care team such as a Social Worker or Respite Carer. Securing the support and cooperation of everyone in this team will be an important step in creating a successful transition, but most of the work – the coordination and communication – invariably lies with those from the settings.

The family will need to agree who can be part of the team, but you can also seek additional advice from those who don't need to be fully involved at every stage. Holding a TAC/TAF meeting as early as possible in the process so that a timetable can be devised, desired outcomes agreed, responsibilities allocated, and support strategies put in place will help you to create a transition plan which can then be reviewed and updated at each subsequent meeting.

Who? (child, parent, sibling, key person)	Area of need (what is important to me)	Support strategies (what helps me)	Start date	Outcome

Strategies that can be considered when building your transition plan could include:

- Create an enabling environment in the new setting which is initially as similar as possible to the old setting.
- Encouraging a Whole School Approach which includes everyone who might come into contact with the child.
- Create a Total Communication Environment throughout the school – not just in the classroom; provide a Social Story for the child including photos of their new school.
- Establish a series of supported visits throughout the summer term with a gradual transfer between key attachment adults.

Don't forget that, just as each child and family is individual, each team will have different members who can contribute strengths, skills and experience to the process, so be sure to use these to give the child every advantage.

A successful transition will need careful attention to timings. It is a good idea to draw up a timeline with the help of members of the Team Around the Child. Populate it with dates of significant events such as visits and meetings, but also with deadlines for the various and multiple pieces of paperwork that might be needed. Keep it somewhere accessible (but confidential) so that it can be a working document. Work backwards from the child's first day in their new setting and think about what needs to happen when. You will probably find that some things need to happen several months ahead regardless of whether or not the school place has been allocated – there may not be enough time in the summer term to get everything in place.

Here are some of the events/significant dates you could mark on the timeline: allocation of school place; initial TAC meeting and reviews; training by external agencies, e.g. community nursing; visit by Occupational Therapist to assess need for specialist seating; funding deadlines.

And here are some pieces of paperwork that you may need help with and so should plan ahead for: individual risk assessment; care plan; one-page profile; education, health and care plan.

Case study: transitioning from Dingley's Promise to a mainstream school

TK attended Dingley's Promise for a year prior to turning school age. Upon school allocations, his parents were unsuccessful in their hope for a specialist school placement and were offered a place within a mainstream school. The parents were anxious about this transition as they were still uncertain that this was the right environment for him; their initial conversations with the school unfortunately did not provide any reassurance, and with agreement with the local authority TK remained at Dingley's Promise for the autumn term. During this term, a new headteacher joined the school, and the parents shared their initial concerns. They made the parents feel at ease and ensured them that they were an inclusive school and agreed a place for TK to start in the reception class with one-to-one support.

It was agreed that TK would join his reception class in January at the start of the spring term, on a reduced timetable – which allowed the school time to adapt the environment and send staff on training to meet TK's needs. The new head worked closely with Dingley's Promise, coordinating meetings with the family and utilising our expertise and knowledge of TK to ensure a robust transition takes place. Dingley's Promise team members completed multiple transition visits with TK to support him in his new setting environment, coaching and mentoring his new one-to-one on interventions and strategies on how to best support TK's needs.

This close collaboration and knowledge sharing enabled TK to transition seamlessly into his new school with the right support in place and continue accessing learning alongside his peers. Seeing good inclusive practice in place enables school staff to feel confident and comfortable in continuing these practices in their own classrooms and have since seen the positive impact of strategies implemented on not just TK but other children within his class.

Conclusion

It is important to remember that at the core of the process is the child with their individual strengths and needs. A well-supported and valued family can offer a web of consistency, and building a trusting relationship with them throughout the transition will help to establish a solid base for future partnership as the child progresses through the school. The Team Around the Child can bring multiple skills and competencies to the process, but like any team, it needs to be effectively managed to ensure that every member of the group feels encouraged to contribute and pull together for the sake of the child.

Reflecting on what worked well in the transition process and what was less successful will help you adjust transition plans for future children with SEND. You will also learn about your own strengths and identify continuing professional development needs. You can celebrate success with the team, strengthening partnerships for future joint working, and you may even identify aspects of your setting that are more inclusive as a result of the transition process.

> **Reflection time**
>
> How do you share the child's strengths, skills and interests with their new setting or school?
>
> Who is involved in supporting a child with SEND to transition to their new setting or school?
>
> When do you start your transition process? Are you the voice of the child? Do you advocate for their need for an enhanced transition which may look different to that of their peers?

References and further reading

Ecological Theory: Bronfenbrenner's Five Systems [Available at: https://www.explorepsychology.com/ecological-theory/].

Maslow's Hierarchy of Needs [Available at: https://www.simplypsychology.org/maslow.html].

SEND Code of Practice: 0 to 25 Years – GOV.UK [Available at: https://www.gov.uk/government/publications/send-code-of-practice-0-to-25].

12
Well-being in early years

Louise White

> **KEY DEFINITIONS**
>
> Well-being: The state of being comfortable, healthy and happy. It encompasses physical, emotional and social factors and impacts both children and adults.
>
> Co-regulation: Adults guiding children through emotional and behavioural responses, providing necessary support and modelling appropriate reactions. For children with SEND, co-regulation might require more individualised approaches, considering each child's unique sensory, cognitive, and emotional needs.
>
> Self-regulation: The child's ability to manage their own emotions and behaviours, a skill that can be particularly challenging for children with SEND due to differences in emotional processing, communication abilities or sensory sensitivities.

Introduction

When we consider well-being in early years, it is important to remember that everyone's well-being should be supported. This includes children, parents/carers and educators who work with children. Poor well-being impacts people's ability to interact, engage, concentrate and care for themselves and those around them, and so the well-being of one person within the circle can negatively impact those they are around them. This chapter will explore how well-being impacts children and those around them and the ways in which we can support children, families and the wider team..

Understanding the well-being of children

Well-being refers to the overall health and happiness of a person; this may include emotional, physical and social factors. For children in the early years, well-being is crucial as it lays the foundation for their future development. When thinking about well-being in young children, we should consider:

1. **Physical Health:** Ensuring children have access to nutritious food, regular physical activity, and health services.
2. **Emotional and Mental Health:** Providing a safe and supportive environment where children can express their feelings and develop emotional resilience.
3. **Social Development:** Encouraging positive interactions with peers and adults to build social skills and relationships.
4. **Cognitive Development:** Stimulating learning through play and educational experiences to support brain development.
5. **Safety and Security:** Creating a secure environment where children feel protected and cared for.

Promoting well-being in early childhood helps children develop the skills, values and behaviours they need to thrive both now and in the future. Creating the templates for successful transitions to school, healthy adult relationships, positive life outcomes and enjoyment. For children with SEND, all these factors can be impacted by their needs, making it critical that we consider the child's well-being throughout the support process.

When children experience poor well-being, such as having poor physical health, inadequate social support or when they experience poor emotional regulation, their bodies often react with a stress response. Immediate impacts of a stress response include an increased heart rate, elevated blood pressure and heightened alertness. However, when the body's stress response is activated too regularly or continuously, this can lead to toxic stress, which can have a severe and long-lasting impact on the child's physical and emotional health. Toxic stress can disrupt brain development, impair cognitive functions and increase the risk of chronic health issues such as heart disease, diabetes and mental health disorders. Not only are children with SEND more likely to suffer from poor well-being, but poor well-being can also impact children's needs and create circumstances in which children require further support.

It is important that we recognise contributing factors to poor well-being in children as the long-term effects can impact them for the rest of their lives.

- Physical health issues such as chronic illnesses or poor nutrition can cause the body to be in a constant state of stress, leading to increased levels of stress hormones like cortisol. For children with SEND, it is important to work with medical professionals involved to ensure that we are providing the correct support so as not to exacerbate illnesses and medical needs.
- Emotional and mental health challenges can activate the body's stress response, making it difficult for children to cope with everyday challenges. Recognising mental health issues in children in the early years can be challenging, as children are still learning to understand their emotions and regulate themselves. However, it is important to understand the impacts of unmet emotional needs and the importance of providing strong emotional support to children at this time in their lives.
- Difficulties understanding and navigating social situations and relationships may lead children to feel isolated and vulnerable. Children with SEND may have their own

challenges around integrating themselves with their peers, but can also experience discrimination and rejection from their peers due to being different.

Supporting children's well-being

One way in which we can have a huge impact on children's well-being is understanding and supporting their ability to navigate their emotions and regulate themselves. In early years settings, promoting co- and self-regulation requires a thoughtful, individualised approach. By creating supportive environments and providing tailored opportunities for emotional growth, educators can support children to develop the skills for managing their emotions and behaviours, which builds greater independence, resilience and confidence and the skills needed to thrive.

Many children, particularly autistic children, find it hard to understand, express, and regulate their emotions. As a result, they may display distressed behaviours to communicate that they are feeling stressed or anxious, and as a means of calming themselves. To support them with this behaviour, we can give them the understanding and tools they need to express their emotions in a more appropriate way, as well as help them develop ways to calm down when they become dysregulated.

Possible reasons for this need	*Examples of emotional and regulation behaviours*
- The child doesn't have the emotional vocabulary or understanding to verbally communicate their emotions - The child finds it difficult to calm when they feel stressed, worried, angry or confused	- Throwing, hitting, kicking or biting - Repeating actions such as hand flapping, tapping, bouncing up and down - Crying, babbling, not settling into a calmer state for a long period of time

Developing individualised support plans that include specific strategies for emotional regulation can help us tailor our approach to each child's needs. These plans may incorporate sensory resources, specific calming techniques or communication strategies.

Visual supports, such as emotion card, social stories or communication boards, can support children to understand and manage their emotions. They provide a visual representation of abstract concepts like feelings and appropriate responses. Creating a 'regulation station' such as the one shown in Figure 12.1 offers the child a constant opportunity to engage in this way and explore their emotions through play.

Establishing a strong, trusting relationship is important. Children often need extra time and consistency to feel comfortable and understood. Gentle, patient communication and positive reinforcement can build trust and encourage open emotional expression.

As educators, we must be attuned to each child's signals, recognising both verbal and non-verbal communication cues. This responsiveness allows for timely and appropriate co-regulation interventions, helping to de-escalate potential emotional times.

Figure 12.1 Regulation Station

Teach words/signs/gestures that describe emotions

Emotions and emotional vocabulary can be difficult to understand. For example, what is the difference between worried and anxious? What is the difference between calm and happy? Lots of children find recognising and labelling their own emotions difficult, and if they find it too hard, may give up verbally expressing their feelings altogether. Use every opportunity you can to label how you, the child and others might be feeling, choosing simple vocabulary (happy, sad, angry). Label staff and child's emotions to the child when you see it – for example: "Leah is smiling; she must be feeling happy today"; "You are talking loudly; I think you might be feeling angry". Also encourage children to think about how characters in books may be feeling. This will help to build their emotional knowledge and increase their confidence in expressing themselves. A set of emotions symbols or pictures may help, as well as using Makaton signs to visually show the emotion.

Calming techniques

When a child's behaviour seems to be communicating that they feel upset, confused, anxious, or angry, it is important that you help them to calm before doing anything else. This will help to prevent, reduce or stop distressed behaviour. If you know the child well, you may already know of some activities they will find calming. For children you don't know well, it may be worth observing them while they are calm. What activities do they enjoy most? In what situations do they seem most calm? It is important that verbal communication is limited as the quieter and calmer you can be, the quieter and calmer they will become.

Concentrate on your breathing; even making enhanced or loud long and slow breaths may help the child calm. Having a calm basket with activities and toys that help the child to calm down available nearby may also help. Some children may take a long time to calm, so try not to rush the child into the next activity once they seem more relaxed. Give them longer to calm than you think they are going to need.

Offering choices, but in a structured and clear manner, helps children feel empowered and in control. Choices should be limited to avoid overwhelming the child, and they should be presented in a straightforward way, often using visuals or simple language.

Encouraging small steps towards independence, such as self-care tasks or participation in group activities, helps build confidence and self-regulation skills. These opportunities should be scaffolded according to the child's abilities and gradually increased as the children develop these skills. For children with sensory processing difficulties, providing access to sensory resources like fidget toys, noise cancelling headphones or weighted blankets can help them self-regulate. These resources can support managing sensory input and maintaining focus.

Teaching children simple emotion regulation techniques, such as introducing calm boxes, counting, or using a sensory calm space, can empower them to manage their emotions. These resources should be used regularly and integrated into our daily routine.

Providing a quiet retreat, such as a book corner, cosy corner, dark den, or a giant box, can create a quiet retreat. Bring in added sensory toys, resources such as a choice of cushions or blankets that they can go to independently or with their key person at times when they feel overwhelmed. On overwhelming days, focus on reducing the demand and increasing calming opportunities, such as some calm music, deep pressure massage, dark spaces with sensory lights, or offering some physical activities such as pushing, pulling, jumping, spinning or swinging.

Addressing sensory difficulties through a sensory diet benefits children by giving regular opportunities to meet a child's sensory needs throughout the day. This could be a physical activity, safe objects that can be mouthed, or calming experiences. We know that many children with sensory processing difficulties are often on high alert all day, which can trigger multiple meltdowns.

The purpose of a calm box is to support a child who is feeling an intense emotion such as anger, frustration or who is feeling overwhelmed. Calm boxes are simple but useful resources that can be used for a variety of children or tailored to the individual child. When a child is feeling an intense emotion and struggling to regulate themselves, the objects in the calm box can be used to support them in finding their emotional balance. The objects used in a calm box will meet a range of sensory needs, such as playdough, fidget toys, a textured or weighted ball and bubbles.

Within our centres we may have calm boxes that are freely accessible to all children as well as some specifically made with the interest of children in mind. Specific boxes are clearly labelled with a photograph of the child to support them and their peers in recognising their individual possessions. Once a child is familiar with using a calm box, having one that is easy and clear to access at all times of the day promotes their sense of confidence and security in knowing that objects that bring them calm and comfort are not too far away.

The development of co- and self-regulation skills in children can really enhance their emotional awareness and adaptability. As children become more attuned to their emotional states and learn effective regulation strategies, this can support social situations more effectively, help them cope with sensory challenges, and enable them to participate more in educational and social activities.

These skills also support a child's ability to handle change and adversity. By learning to self-regulate, children can become more resilient, better equipped to deal with the unexpected and more capable of developmental progress.

 Case study: K's journey at Dingley's Promise

At Dingley's Promise, we recognise that well-being is the foundation for all learning. When children join our sessions, we prioritise a smooth transition, focusing on building trusting relationships and emotional security, before introducing any educational goals.

In January 2025, K joined our Reading centre. She has a diagnosis of cerebral palsy, global developmental delay and truncal hypotonia. K faced significant challenges with communication, social interaction and emotional regulation. Initially, she would cry when leaving her mother and became visibly upset if her key person left the room. She avoided eye contact with other practitioners and often sought security in our "scoot" – a familiar, enclosed space she used as a safe zone. K would refuse to come out of the scoot or allow her key person, to move away from her side.

K preferred solitary play and would shy away from interacting with her peers. Transitions between activities or spaces within the setting were particularly distressing for her. She relied heavily on gestures and visual supports to communicate.

Intent

To create a safe, consistent, and trusting environment that supports K's emotional well-being, which in turn enables K to feel secure enough to engage, build relationships and begin learning.

Implementation

To support her, we ensured the scoot was always available during her sessions, helping her feel safe and in control within her new environment. A consistent key person was assigned to her. Through a predictable routine, calm communication, and sensitive, attuned interactions, her key person developed a strong and trusting relationship with K. She used visual aids, a gentle tone, and close observation to learn about K's play preferences and emotional cues.

As K gradually became more settled, other staff members began engaging with her alongside the key person. They would introduce toys during her play and model fun, engaging interactions – gently encouraging small interactions and shared enjoyment. These small, intentional moments helped K begin to build confidence with other practitioners. Over time, her key person was able to take a step back, allowing K to develop trusting relationships with other staff members.

Impact

Eventually, K felt secure enough to come out of the scoot. We were able to replace it with one of her favourite activities: water play. She began accessing this independently with her key person and, with growing curiosity and joy, started crawling around the playroom. Movement became a source of fun and exploration.

Today, K is a confident and happy member of our setting. She interacts comfortably with all staff, no longer requires the scoot for reassurance, and transitions smoothly through our daily routine. Her bond with her key person remains strong, and she has developed meaningful connections with other educators. With her emotional needs met, K is now thriving in her learning journey.

Understanding family resilience

Family resilience considers the aspects that make up resilience, how they might affect families and what steps settings can take to build those core aspects of resilience. We also look at attachment theory and consider how we can help families where there are attachment difficulties. Sometimes these may be related to SEND, sometimes now, but it is critical for the well-being of a young child to have secure attachments. The stronger our families are, the more likely their children will be happy, therefore any actions we can take in the early years to build this, will have a positive impact on a child's well-being.

Family resilience refers to the collective strengths and adaptive capacities of a family unit, which enable them to cope with and recover from challenges.

Key aspects of family resilience would include the ability of a family to adjust to changes; managing their emotions, particularly when under stress, whether they arise from everyday challenges or significant crises; the emotional closeness and support among family members that gives a sense of unity and togetherness; having effective communication within the family, which facilitates understanding, problem-solving and emotional sharing and support; and access to supportive relationships that are outside the immediate family, including friends, extended family, and also within the community they live.

Families need to build the ability to identify, access and effectively use external and internal resources that are on offer and know what is available to them.

These things work together to create a resilient family that can provide stability and support for children. When families are resilient, they can better support their children's developmental needs, even in the face of challenges.

The well-being of young children is deeply influenced by the resilience of their families, as family stability enables children to experience consistent emotional support, which in turn builds trust and security. Parents are the children's role models, and where they demonstrate effective strategies, children learn and adopt emotional regulation skills.

Resilient families create environments where children feel safe to explore and learn, leading to cognitive and social development.

In contrast, families that struggle with resilience may inadvertently expose children to increased stress and instability, which can affect their emotional and behavioural development. Early years settings have a critical role in supporting these families, enhancing their capacity for resilience and, consequently, improving child outcomes.

Supporting family resilience in early years settings

Early years educators and family support workers can support family resilience via information and strategies, providing a foundation for healthy child development.

Building strong partnerships with families and maintaining regular, open communication helps build trust and encourages collaboration. This can include newsletters, meetings with parents and informal conversations.

Recognising and respecting the diverse cultural backgrounds and values of families ensures inclusive and respectful practices, strengthening the partnership between us and our families.

Offering information sessions on topics such as parenting strategies, child development and more, alongside building connections with other families, connecting families with local resources, such as mental health services, financial support or community support groups, provides additional support and has a positive impact on a family.

By hosting events such as coffee mornings/afternoons, social evenings, information sessions and other parent engagement sessions, you can provide families with the opportunity to connect with each other, share their experiences, and create a network of support among each other. Parents of children with SEND often report that isolation is a major issue for them, and if you are able to link these parents, it will have a huge effect on their well-being – maybe even creating friendships that last a lifetime. Recently, we heard of a family who had met others when they were accessing one of our Dingley's Promise centres almost 40 years ago. When faced with his wife's serious illness, it was the parents which the husband had met at our setting that helped him through, showing just how life-changing those early parental friendships can be.

Providing a safe space for parents to discuss their challenges can offer much-needed emotional support and practical advice in the moment. Where you are able to provide resources and offer training or insight into their child's emotional development in the home, you can equip parents with the strategies needed to confidently support their child. This includes teaching parents about emotion recognition, effective communication and consistent behavioural strategies.

Well-being in early years 155

You might find that appointing a team member as a dedicated parent champion will enable you to provide consistent opportunities to engage families and share information to support them at home.

In order to cope with supporting their child's behaviour and emotional development, families are going to need resilience. Resilience means an ability to accept life's challenges, to believe in your ability to cope and adapt, and to quickly move past failures, learning from mistakes and being willing to try again. As well as emotional support, the family may also benefit from practical help. The more space you can help them to create in their day, the more likely they are to be able to implement supportive strategies for their child's behaviour.

Help for families may include: finding out if they are entitled to any benefits and helping them to fill in the forms; finding grants to help low-income families who are raising a disabled child; helping them to apply for respite or short breaks (Local Offer); finding advice about sleep or other common difficulties for children with SEND and sharing it in an easy-to-understand way; signposting to parent information courses or support groups as demonstrated in Figure 12.2 through the Dingley's Promise family outreach service.

Figure 12.2 Information sharing with families

Well-being of the team

Creating a culture of psychological safety is a great starting point. Psychological safety is a culture of trust and confidence which enables everyone within your team to be able to share their vulnerabilities, as well as seek help and support without the fear of negative consequences or being left to deal with it alone. Often, this is the point where staff begin to question "Is this the career for me?" or "Am I good enough?". Sometimes these are questions they may feel confident to ask whether that's in a supervision or conversation, but more commonly, they keep these to themselves, internalising them in a negative way.

Having a place of work where well-being plays a large part can help you and your entire team to have the confidence to offload and seek support. When thinking about well-being we are thinking about every aspect, including support from management, support from their peers, the environment itself and the external support that can be accessed and signposted to. Well-being is a team effort where it's imperative that everyone is aware of what is available to them, not only so they can access it, but also to be able to share should a colleague choose to confide in them.

Within settings, commonly there are multiple rooms leading to sub-teams being formed within the larger staff team. This can create "support pockets" where the team feel particularly safe to share worries, concerns, etc., and can be the first stepping stone for support. Staff being able to support each other enables that initial voice to be heard, and can also prevent any potential anxiety of feeling that they have to ask their manager for support. Sometimes peer-to-peer support can be the best tool as they can understand the situation the individual finds themselves in and would know what to suggest to resolve it, preventing isolation within the team.

When a staff member comes to you as their manager for support, it's imperative that we make time to listen and take on board what they are saying about how they feel. As a manager, it prompts them to reflect and think about the potential triggers; could these be avoided?

When we think about the environment itself, we need to think about where our staff can go for five minutes if they need to remove themselves when they become overwhelmed. Quiet spaces at work, whether they are for taking a break, doing some work, etc., are really useful. Not being able to access something like this could have a detrimental effect on their mental health and well-being. Consider implementing "hall passes"; this could be a card kept on the whiteboard or a small item kept on a shelf that your team picks up to signify they are overwhelmed and need a moment. This can sometimes be easier than verbalising when they are finding a situation challenging.

Let's think about external support and how we can signpost these services to our teams. The use of posters, leaflets, newsletters, etc., shows that there is a way for your team to have access to public health and well-being information. Being visible and accessible means that all staff can access it without having to go out and search, which can be a daunting task. Having resources, well-being information, and advice also leads to the reduction in the negative stigma that surrounds mental health, particularly in a setting where there are clear, practical procedures in place to promote mental health and well-being. This also reiterates your culture of psychological safety and gives your team the confidence to seek external support if needed. It can also open up dialogue between leaders and staff members, offering the opportunity for further advice, support or simply a listening ear. You may have members of the team who may not wish to talk, and with this in mind it is important to enable your team to access support information and contact details confidentially, without having to speak to their colleagues, this may be something they want to do alone and may share with you once they feel more confident.

Managers are often excellent at supporting their team's well-being and mental health, but at times are not so good at looking after their own. It is important that when sharing the information on external support, leaders take note of this information and actively use it to protect their own mental health and well-being. Question what is readily available for the managers to access, and does it differ from what is offered to the wider team? Teams will learn from how their managers deal with pressure, and this can become an unspoken way of working. If a leader is neglecting their mental health and well-being, it is likely their team will do the same.

Conclusion

Supporting the well-being of families, children and your colleagues may feel like a daunting prospect, but you are not on this journey alone. Working together and learning from each other can help you to create safe spaces for children, families and team members to share their stressors and challenges and navigate ways to reduce and face these. Remember you cannot resolve or remove everybody's challenges, but you can be a listening ear, a judgement-free voice and a signposter of services, to promote well-being.

References and further reading

Allingham, S. (2020) *Emotional literacy in the early years: Helping children balance body and mind (Little Steps)*. London, Practical Pre-School Books.

Conkbayir, M. (2022) *The neuroscience of the developing child: Self-regulation for wellbeing and a sustainable future*. London, Routledge.

Department for Education (2023) *Mental health for early years children* [Available at: https://help-for-early-years-providers.education.gov.uk/health-and-wellbeing/mental-health-for-early-years-children].

Douglas-Osborn, E. et al. (2021) *Early Years staff wellbeing: A resource for managers and teams* [Available at: https://www.annafreud.org/resources/under-fives-wellbeing/early-years-staff-wellbeing-a-resource-for-managers-and-teams/].

Education Endowment Foundation, Grocott, L. (2024) *Supporting children's mental health and wellbeing in the early years* [Available at: https://educationendowmentfoundation.org.uk/early-years/mental-health-wellbeing].

Moxley, K. (n.d.) 'A beginners guide to: Educator wellbeing'. *Tapestry Beginners Guides* [Available at: https://tapestry.info/beginners-guides/].

Sisera, C. (2024) *Early years wellbeing: Where to focus to make the biggest impact* [Available at: https://nationalcollege.com/news/early-years-wellbeing-where-to-focus-to-make-the-biggest-impact#:~:text=Supporting%20Mental%20Health%20and%20Resilience,environment%20that%20prioritises%20mental%20wellbeing].

IN CONCLUSION

Throughout this book we have explored the importance of inclusion. Developing inclusive practice, environments and approaches, and recognising and valuing each child as an individual are essential. Making a conscious decision to provide a space in which all children are supported to not only access but thrive is vital to ensure equitable involvement in education. As you develop your inclusive provision, remember:

- **Every Child Is Unique:** Time should be taken to observe, gather information and understand who that child is. This will enable you to implement strategies of support that are relevant and beneficial for that child.
- **Use Celebratory Language:** Recognising a child's strengths, skills and interests provides you with the best foundations for a positive outlook for the child, their family and educators who work with them. This creates a positive awareness of themselves, contributing to healthy mental wellbeing.
- **There Is a Team Around the Child:** Supporting children with SEND is not a one-person job; there is, and should be, a range of professionals and family members working together to implement the right support at the right time for the child. Share goals and strategies to ensure you are providing a consistent approach in the setting, at home and as they transition to school.
- **Plan and Prepare Your Provision:** Planning to support children with SEND ensures you can confidently offer places for children to access their full entitlement. This includes understanding your local population and community, working with your local authority to access the correct funding and support, and creating a welcoming and inviting setting through your inclusive vision and values.

All children can and should have the opportunity to experience inclusion and, as caring, compassionate and dedicated early years educators, we can make that happen for them. Creating places where children's behaviours are recognised and understood for the messages they are trying to share, where children's differing methods of communication are encouraged and heard, and varying needs are noticed and responded to in the moment, will all contribute to giving children the tools to succeed and have a positive start to their educational journey.

160 In conclusion

We are in a position to recognise and implement support for children at the earliest stages of their development, equipping them with the tools to confidently navigate their needs as they access the world around them. By being reflective, we can adapt and adjust to ensure the support we are providing meets the needs of the child, and consider how our environment and approaches are providing the right opportunities for all children in our care.

Inclusion is everybody's responsibility and you play an important role in shaping the lives of the children who walk through your door. Make every day count, with an dedicated focus on inclusion which gives every child the opportunity to fulfil their potential and the best possible start to their educational journey.

INDEX

accessibility 10, 105-106; building 4; play space 110; slide 8
active listening 57, 90
adopted children with SEND 99
adult response audit 123, *124*
adverse childhood experiences 99; attachment and 34
adverts, recruitment 75-76
Alternative and Augmentative Communication (AAC) devices 62
aspiration 2
Assess, Plan, Do, Review cycle 6-8
assessment 37; baseline 38; characteristics of effective teaching and learning (COeTL) 39; children with SEND 6, 7, 28, 29; deficit-based approach 45; DfE guidance and toolkit 48; early years foundation stage profile 38; frameworks 39; language of 45-47; Leuven scale 40, 41-42; methods 39; observation 38, 39, 46; one-page profile 42; progress check at age 2 38, 50; reception baseline 38; sensory and physical needs 52; strengths-based 39, 45-46; summative 38; Support and Achievement Play Plans (SAPPs) 47, 48-50; toolkit 51; working with families 42, 43-44, 45; working with professionals 44-45
attachment: adverse childhood experiences and 34; insecure 31-32; secure 31, 153; strategies for supporting 34-35
attainment gap, children with SEND 137
attention deficit hyperactivity disorder (ADHD) 118, 119
attention skills, SPD and 118
attention-seeking behaviour, responding to 126
audit: adult response 123, *124*; environment and routines 123
authoritarian parents 89
authoritative parents 89

autistic children: brain connections in 119; challenging behaviours 131-132; development 120; gender identity 100; non-verbal communication 56; transitions 131
auxiliary aids and services 5

barriers: to inclusion 3; to transitions 140-141
baseline assessment 38
baskets 40
behaviour/s 54, 55; adult response audit 123; attention-seeking 126; biting 131; calming 150-151; challenging 131-132; communicating fundamental needs 130; confusion/uncertainty, responding to 129-130; coping mechanisms 101; dangerous 123; delayed social skills 127, 128; distressed 124-125; environmental audit 123; fight/flight/freeze/fawn or flop response 116; iceberg metaphor 116-117; impulsive 117, 118; influences on 115-116; intent 117; masking 98; overstimulation 127; sensory needs 127; STAR approach 122-123; Support Plan 131; support strategies 119-120, 124-125; triggers 121-122; TRUST tool 121; *see also* emotions/emotional
bias, educator 88
biting 131
body language 54, 55, 56; eye contact 57, 85; intensive interaction 65; mirroring 89
boundaries, play space 112
brain: autistic 119; early years development 119; functional areas *118*; networks 118, 119; in people with ADHD 118, 119
brainstem 32
Bronfenbrenner, Urie, Ecological Systems Theory 141-142
buildings, accessibility 4

business planning for inclusion 15; market research 16; reasons for higher SEND enrolment 16-17; understanding the local SEND population 16

calculating your potential income 17-18
calm boxes 34, 108, 151
carers 81; role in child's EY transition to school 141, 142-144
celebratory approach 37, 82, 95
challenging behaviours 131-132; support for families in the home environment 134; understanding the context 133, 134
challenging conversations 81, 88; active listening 90; barriers 87, 91-92; body language 89; celebratory approach 82; empathy 90; environment 86, 87; recognising different styles of parenting 89; unplanned 91
changes, planned and unplanned 129
characteristics of effective teaching and learning (COeTL) 39
Childcare Act 2006 16
Childcare Sufficiency Assessment (CSA) 16
child-centred approach 109
children with SEND: adopted 99; assessment 6, 7, 29, 30; attainment gap 137; communication challenges 56-57; coping mechanisms 101; dysregulation 107; EAL speakers 30-31; eating disorders 101; emotional regulation, supporting 149; engagement 39; feelings of isolation 101; gender differences 98-99; insecure attachment 33; intersections 96; in the local population 16-17; mental health issues 101; resilience 139; self-help skills 138-139; settling-in sessions 84; siblings 82; targets 6; transition process 19; transition to school 137-138; well-being, supporting 149; *see also* behaviour
cognition and learning needs 8; strategies for supporting 11-13
collaboration/collaborative 7; across services 18-19, 20; approach to transitions 141, 142-144, 145; assessment 42, 43-44; with local authority 19, 20; with specialists 44-45; team 71
communication 7, 8, 54; active listening 57; Alternative and Augmentative Communication (AAC) devices 62; autistic children 56; behaviour 55; body language 89; buttons 64; celebratory approach 82; challenges for children with SEND 56-57; consistent 58; diaries 84-85; distractions 57, 58; of emotions 55; eye contact 57, 85; fundamental needs 130; gestures 7, 56; knock, knock what's in the box? 65; of needs 124; newsletters 85; online 85; provocations 61; -rich environment 57, 62; signing 58; situational understanding 59; social media 85; strategies for supporting 11-13; team 72; through play 59, 61-62, 64-65; tools 62; unplanned conversations 91; visual aids 58, 59, 62, 63, 64, 66; visual symbol book 66; vocalisations 56; *see also* challenging conversations; engagement; interaction; verbal communication
communication board 9, 62; *see also* visual aids
community cupboard 98
community events, communicative opportunities 86
confusion/uncertainty, responding to 129-130
consistent communication 59
coping mechanisms, in children with SEND 101
coping skills 139
core stability 7
co-regulation 147, 152
cortical system 33
crawling 7-8
Crenshaw, Kimberlé, intersectionality 96
curriculum, inclusive 20-21

deficit-based approach 45
delayed social skills, responding to 127, 128
demographics, local SEND population 16-17
design, outdoor environment 111
development 37, 39, 102-103; autistic children 120; brain 119; monitoring 52; social skill 127, 128
Development Matters Guidance 33
DfE Early Years SEND Assessment Toolkit 29
diagnosis 1, 8; SEND 98; Syndrome Without a Name (SWAN) 26; *see also* early identification of need
Dingley's Promise 9, 20, 26, 39, 45, 65, 84, 152; DfE Early Years SEND Assessment Toolkit 29; family support 94; getting to know your team form 77; outdoor environment 111, *112*; transition to school 145
Disability Access Fund (DAF) 17
Disability Living Allowance (DLA) 17-18
discrimination 96; racial 100
distractions 58, *59*

distressed behaviour, creating support strategies 124-125
documents: Childcare Sufficiency Assessment (CSA) 16; Ordinarily Available Provision (OAP) 3, 106; Support and Achievement Play Plan (SAPP) 44
double consciousness 100
drop off/pick up, communicating during 84
dysregulation 107; *see also* challenging behaviours; emotions/emotional

early identification of need 24; attachment issues 32-34; distinguishing SEND from other needs 34-35; educator benefits 26-27; family benefits 26; impact of support 27-28; implementation of support 27; parent engagement 28, 29; prenatal 28; role of educators 29
Early Years Foundation Stage (EYFS): enabling environment 104-105; key person 9, 55, 66, 71. *See also* key person; profile 38; progress check at age 2 50
eating disorders 101
echolalia 56-57
educator: benefits of early identification 25-26; bias 88; "hall passes" 156; meeting with parents 84; paperwork 37-38; role in early identification 29; team 68; training 9
emotions/emotional: communicating 55; co-regulation 147, 152; helping children with SEND in communicating 149; intelligence 34, 42; labelling 150; negative 140; regulation 107, 116, 124; security 142-143; self-regulation 107, 108, 119, 147, 151, 152; vocabulary 150; well-being 152
empathy 88, 90
enabling environment 104-105; relationships 109
engagement: children with SEND 39; family 91-92; parental 27, 28, 84-85, 86
English as an Additional Language (EAL): children, supporting 29, 30-31; families, supporting 86; *see also* communication
environment 2-3, 114; accessibility 4, 105-106, 110; auditing 123; for challenging conversations 86, 87; communication-rich 57, 62; enabling 104-105; floor plan 105-106; gender-affirming 100; height adjustments 106; home learning 93-94; inclusive 105; indoor 109-110; outdoor 110-111; quiet retreat 151; quiet spaces 156; reasonable adjustments. See reasonable adjustments; regulation station 149; resourcing 110; routines 112; safe space 83, 107, 112, 152-153; sense of belonging 2, 140-141; supporting sensory and physical needs 107, 108; sustainable 113; total communication 106, 107; *see also* play space; transitions
environmental audit 105
equality 1
Equality Act 2010 4, 105
equity 1
eye contact 57, 85

facial expressions 56, 57; intensive interaction 65
family/ies 22, 81; benefits of early identification 25; challenging conversations 86, 87, 88; engaging 28, 29, 91-92; with financial needs, supporting 97-98; glass children 83; home visits 85; information sharing 56, 72; LGBTQIA+ 100; "living grief" 102; meetings 134; providing support 84-85, 95; resilience 153-155; role in child's EY transition to school 141, 142-144; sharing assessments with 43, 44-45, 46; siblings of children with SEND 83-84; steering/advisory groups 85; understanding their personal experiences 82; *see also* challenging conversations; parent/s
fight/flight/freeze/fawn or flop response 116
financial aid 5
floor plan 105-106
food bank, vouchers 98
Forest Schools 111
frameworks: assessment 39; Early Years Foundation Stage (EYFS) 9, 51, 56, 67, 72, 104
functional areas of the brain *118*
fundamentals of inclusion 3, 9-10
funding 17-18
fundraising 18; communicative opportunities 85

games, knock, knock what's in the box? 65
gender: -affirming environment 99; answering questions about 99; -neutral language 99; and SEND 98-99
genetic testing 26, 28
gestures 7, 56; for emotions 150
glass children 82
graduated approach 6-8
grants 17
guidance: assessment 47; special education needs 70

"hall passes" 156
hearing aid, microphone transmitter 6
height adjustments, play environment 106
High Needs Block (HNB) 18
high-quality teaching 4
home learning: educator support 92–93; sustainable practices 93
home visits 84
hygge approach 22
hyperflexia 26
hypersensitivity 118

identity 96; gender 98; LGBTQIA+ 99; racial 100
impulsive behaviour 117, 118
inclusion/inclusive 1, 2, 8; barriers 3; business planning 16, 17–18; consistent 2; curriculum 20–21; EAL children 30–31; environment 105. *See also* enabling environment; fundamentals 3, 9–10; team approach 69–71
inclusive practice 2, 105, 114; during child' EY transition to school 145; collaboration across services 18–19, 20; continuous development 73; influences 21
income, calculating 17–18
independence, promoting 138–139, 151; *see also* behaviour
indoor environment 109–110
inequality 96; racial 100
information sharing: with families 42, 43–44, 71; with local authority 19; with parents 154–155; with professionals 44; *see also* communication; meetings
insecure attachment 31–32
interaction 7, 8, 55, 63; challenging conversations 86, 87, 88; delayed social skills 127, 128; intensive 65; provocations 62; strategies for supporting 11–14, 152–153
interoception 107
intersectionality 82, 96
intersections 96, 102–103; gender and SEND 97–98; poverty and SEND 97–98
intervention: graduated approach 6–8; reviewing 6; *see also* early identification of need
interview, team candidate 75

jargon 81, 90
job description, team member 77–78

key person 9, 55, 66, 152–153; roles 71
knock, knock what's in the box? 65

LA (living allowance) 17–18
labelling: emotions 150; resources 110

language: of assessment 46–48; body 55, 56, 57, 65, 86, 90; celebratory 38, 83, 95, 158; gender-neutral 99
lanyards 6, 10
leadership 14, 18, 20, 72; vision 15
learning: dispositions 139; outdoor 110–111; play-based 45; provocations 61
Leuven scale 40; involvement element 41–42; well-being element 41
LGBTQIA+ 99; families, supporting 100
lighting 4
limbic system 32
listening 65; active 57, 90; to the voice of the child 55, 66
"living grief" 102
local authority: Childcare Sufficiency Assessment (CSA) 16; information sharing 19; meetings 19; Ordinarily Available Provision (OAP) 4
love, expressing 33–34

Makaton 6; sign for sleep 60; *see also* visual aids
managers, well-being 156–157; *see also* leadership
Maples, Alicia 82
marginalised persons 96
mark making, provocations 10
masking 98
Maslow, Abraham 140
match +1 64
meetings 154; family 134; local authority 19; networking 19; parent-educator 85; TAC/TAF 143–144; team 72; *see also* communication
mental health: parents of children with SEND 101; recognising issues in children 101, 148–149; support for children and families with SEND 101–102
mesosystem 142
messy play 39
methods of assessment 39
microphone transmitter 6
microsystem 142
mirroring 89
modelling 65, 112
moderate learning difficulties (MLD) 8
monitoring: development 52; transitions 141; well-being of family members 143
Montessori approach 21
Mosaic approach 21
movement sessions 7
multisensory activities 61, 62
music and movement sessions 7, 8, 9–10, 57, 106

National Autistic Society 98
needs: behaviour strategies 119-120; cognition and learning 8; communicating 124; communication and interaction 8; fundamental 130; one-page profile 43, 86, 140; of parents during child's transition to school 138; sensory and/or physical 9; social, emotional and mental health 9; strategies for supporting 11-14; *see also* early identification of need; sensory and physical needs
negative emotions 140
networks: brain 118, 119; support 19
newsletters 85
non-verbal communication: body language 54, 55, 56, 89; eye contact 57, 84; intensive interaction 65; *see also* visual aids

observation 38, 39, 66; monitoring child progress 51; recording 46; schema 40
obstacle course 106
occupancy, income and 17
one-page profile 42, 85, 140
online communication 85
Ordinarily Available Provision 1, 3, 4, 104, 105; funding 18
outdoor environment 110-111; Dingley's Promise 111, *112*; meeting children's physical and sensory needs 112
overstimulation 127

paperwork 37-38, 84; transition 144
parent/s 81; attachment issues 32, 33-34; authoritarian 89; authoritative 89; challenging conversations 86, 87, 88; champion 154-155; difficulties caring for their children with SEND 97; -educator meetings 85; engagement 28, 29, 84-85, 86; with financial needs, supporting 97-98; needs of during child's transition to school 138; permissive 89; role in child's EY transition to school 141, 142-144; settling-in sessions 85; sharing information with 154-155; stay-and-play sessions 84; stress and mental health issues 101; supporting 89, 101-102; uninvolved 89; *see also* challenging conversations
pedagogy, bottom-up 111
permissive parenting 89
planned changes 129
play: -based learning 45; calm boxes 34, 108, 151; communication through 59, 61-62, 64; intensive interaction 65; knock, knock what's in the box? 65; multisensory 61; music and movement sessions 7, 8, 9-10, 106; risky 110-111; schematic 41, 109
play space 114; accessibility 105-106, 110; adjusting height of objects 106; boundaries 112; enabling environment 105-106; obstacle course 106; outdoor 110-111
poor well-being: recognising in children 148-149; stress response 148
positive behavior, praising 126; *see also* behaviour
positive relationships 109
poverty, SEND and 97
praising positive behaviour 126
prenatal identification of need 28
professionals *see* specialist/s
profound and multiple learning difficulties (PMLD) 8; recordable communication buttons 64
progress check at age 2 38, 50
pronunciation, recasting 65
proprioception 108
provocation: mark making 9-10; Seed to Sunflower 61
psychological safety 155, 156

Qualified Teacher Status (QTS) 70
quiet retreat 151
quiet spaces 156

reasonable adjustments 1, 3, 4, 6, 20, 104, 105, 138; requirements 5
recasting 65
reception baseline assessment 38
recordable communication buttons 64
recruitment, team member 74-76, 77-78
reflection 7, 9, 22; on child behavior, tools 121-125; team 73
Reggio Emilia approach 21
regulation, emotional 107, 108, 124, 149, 151
relationships 3, 22, 62; positive 109; trusting 42, 138, 141, 149; *see also* attachment
requirements, SENCO 70
resilience 22, 33-34, 111, 139; family 153-155
reviews 6; intervention 8
risky play 110-111
role-modelling 26-27, 70
rotation schema 51
routines 112, 129; auditing 123; for fundamental needs 130-131

safe space 83, 107, 112, 152-153
Scandinavian Forest Schools 111
schema 40; rotation 51

schematic play 40, 109
Schopler, Eric, iceberg metaphor 116-117
screening, team candidate 75
secure attachment 31, 153
Seed to Sunflower provocation 61
self-help skills 138-139
self-regulation 108, 109, 119, 147, 152, 152
self-worth 3
SEND Code of Practice 8-9, 14, 24, 137
sense of belonging 2, 140-141
senses 107, 108
sensory and physical needs 9, 32, 151; assessment 52; enabling environment 107, 108; overstimulation 127
sensory diet 127
sensory play 26-27
sensory processing differences (SPD) 118
setting, communication-rich 57, 62; see also environment
settling-in sessions 84
severe learning difficulties (SLD) 8
siblings of children with SEND 82-83; role in child's EY transition to school 143-144
signing 112
signs 58
situational understanding 59
skills: attention 118; coping 139; emotional regulation 152. See also emotions/emotional; learning dispositions 139; self-help 138-139; social 127, 128
sleep, Makaton sign 60
slide, accessibility 8
SMART (Specific, Measurable, Achievable, Relevant, Time-Bound) goals 6, 37, 49-50
social, emotional and mental health needs 9; strategies for supporting 11-14
social media, communicative opportunities 85
social stories 129-130
special education needs and disabilities (SEND): gender and 98-99; intersections 102-103; LGBTQIA+ and 99-100; mental health and 101; poverty and 97; race and 100
Special Educational Needs and Disabilities Coordinator (SENCO) 9, 70; requirements 70
specialist/s: collaborating with 44-45; offer 4; role in child's EY transition to school 143-144; Special Educational Needs and Disabilities Coordinator (SENCO) 9, 70
speech: early identification of need 25; role-modelling 26-27
Speech and Language Therapy (SaLT) 44-45

Spinocerebellar Ataxia 18 26
STAR approach 122-123
startle reflex 117
stay-and-play sessions 28, 84, 85
Steiner-Waldorf approach 21-22
strengths-based approach 39
strengths-based assessment 45-46
stress response 148
sub-teams 156
summative assessment 38
support: for children and families with financial challenges 97-98; for children's emotional regulation 149; for children's EY to school transition 137-139, 140, 143-144; for children's well-being 149; English as an Additional Language (EAL) children 29, 30-31; family 83-84, 85, 94, 154-155; home learning 92-93; for LGBTQIA+ families 100; mental health 101-102; networks 19; parental 85, 86, 89; for siblings of children with SEND 82-83
Support and Achievement Play Plans (SAPPs) 43, 47, 48-50
sustainable practices 113; home learning 93
symptoms, masking 98
Syndrome Without a Name (SWAN): impact of support 26-27; implementation of support 26

targeted offer 4
Te Whariki 23
teaching, high-quality 4
team/s: building 76; communication 71; developing a reflective culture 73; getting to know 76, 79; inclusive ethos 69-71, 76, 77; meetings 72; parent champion 154-155; recruitment and retention 74-76, 77-78; roles 69; SENCO 70-71; strengths-based approach 72, 76; sub- 156; support for children's EY transition to school 143-144; training 72; vision 15; well-being 74, 155, 156-157
therapy, speech and language 44-45
timeline, transition 144
timers 59
toolkit, assessment 47
tools, communication 62
total communication environment 106, 107; see also communication; environment
toxic stress 148
training: educator 9; team 72
transitions 2, 19, 136, 140; barriers 140-141; for children with autism 131; collaborative approach 141, 142-144, 145; creating a timeline 144; between EY and school

137-138; monitoring 141; paperwork 144; planning and preparation 137-139, 140, 144; role of the parents and family 141, 142-144; timers 59; well-being and 152-153
trauma-informed practice 34
triggers, behaviour 121-122
TRUST tool 121
trusting relationships 42, 138, 141, 149
two-year check 50

uninvolved parents 89
United Nations Convention on the Rights of the Child (UNCRC), Article 12 54
universal offer 4
unplanned conversations 91

values, inclusive 14
verbal communication: echolalia 56-57; match +1 64; recasting 65; tone 56
vestibular system 108
vision 15, 79

visual aids 29, 58, 59, 60, 62, 63, 64, 65, 149; modelling 65; timetable 112, 129, 131
visual symbol book 66
vocabulary: emotional 150; match +1 64; recasting 65
vocalisations 56, 85; intensive interaction 65; *see also* non-verbal communication
voice of the child 54; building confidence 62; communication methods 63, 64-65; listening to 55, 66; one-page profile 140; *see also* communication

well-being 41, 147; emotional 152; family resilience and 153-155; manager 156-157; poor, recognising in children 148-149; psychological safety 155, 156; quiet spaces 156; team 74, 155, 156-157; and transitions 152-153; in young children 147-148
whole team approach 2

Young Children's Voices Network 54

For Product Safety Concerns and Information please contact our EU
representative GPSR@taylorandfrancis.com
Taylor & Francis Verlag GmbH, Kaufingerstraße 24, 80331 München, Germany

www.ingramcontent.com/pod-product-compliance
Lightning Source LLC
Chambersburg PA
CBHW082100230426
43670CB00017B/2907